HARD NINETY: THE BIRTH, DEATH, AND
AFTERLIFE OF A CHILDHOOD DREAM

Hard Ninety

The Birth, Death, and Afterlife
of a Childhood Dream

CHAD FRISK

To my coaches, teammates, and fans.

Acknowledgments

This book could not have been published without the help of many people.

I'd like to thank my editor Wes Matlock for his careful eye and insightful suggestions, my designer Dana Johnson for his atten-tion to detail and stellar aesthetic sense, and to Frank Workman for being willing to write the forward.

I'd also like to thank the readers whose commentary on early drafts helped me to shape the final version—Mike Rathwell, Luke Marshall, Indy Zoeller, John Stewart, Laela Leonard, Cynthia Lunine, Marcy Crawford, Luke Loranger, and Clete Barrick, whose feedback was unusually comprehensive and helpful. Without their help, this book would be much less readable.

Finally, I'd like to thank Amazon for creating the tools that allow me to send books into the world. This book would not exist without them.

Contents

Foreword

The typical baseball book tells a tale of a rags-to-riches player or team, one that overcomes the "nobody-believed-in-us" doubters and defiantly spits in the face of great adversity before rising to the top in dramatic fashion, all to the cheers of an ever-expand ing bandwagon of fanatical adoration.

This is not that book.

This book tells a different baseball story, one void of tape-measure homers, circus-catches, and late-inning heroics. Instead, it tells the story of one boy's transition from gritty young player to washed-up college burnout.

Frisk captures the essence of the game through his astute eyes and stinging wit by focusing on the people and day-to-day expe riences he had as a ballplayer, from his earliest days in T-Ball to his final years playing college baseball for a truly abysmal Whit man College team.

How bad were the Whitman Missionaries during Frisk's four years there?

I'm an inveterate scanner of box scores, and through the miracle of the internet I've been able to follow the fortunes of my favorite players as they've pursued their athletic passions into college.

By the time Frisk was a college senior, I had quit looking up his team's results.

They broke me of the habit. I saw too many box scores showing that Whitman had not only lost (again), but had given up twenty runs in the process. A team has to be really, really bad to allow twenty runs in a game. Doing so multiple times a season is bottom of the barrel, Peanuts-gang stuff. "Tell your statistics to shut up," Charlie Brown famously told Lucy after another hapless season. I'm sure Frisk and his Whitman teammates would have understood what he meant.

Continuing to return to the field after losing so often and so convincingly calls into question the very intelligence of the players attending an institution best known for its academic rigors.

It also serves as a reminder of the powerful lure of our nation's pastime.

Frisk describes his on-again/off-again love affair with the game. His introspective mind has caused him to question (numerous times) the sense and sanity of continuing to love a sport that failed to return his devotion, a situation exacerbated by the damp and chilly spring—and early summer—climate the Pacific Northwest is known for.

But his dogged determination to see his senior season through to the bitter end, in spite of suffering a potentially near-fatal brain injury his junior year, reveals all one needs to know about the lure of the game, if not his character, commitment, and dedication.

Whatever his own conclusions, this humble writer says he's not done loving baseball. Twenty years from now, if I'm still around, I'd love to read Frisk's telling of his own children's experience playing the sport that he was so devoted to.

As Jim Bouton wrote at the conclusion of his breakthrough masterpiece *Ball Four*....

"You spend a good piece of your life gripping a baseball and in the end it turns out that it was the other way around all the time."

—Frank Workman
12/31/2018

This is a memoir, which means that it's almost a work of fiction.

I've done my best to accurately represent my memories. Even if I've managed to do so, however, they are still almost assuredly flawed—not to mention one-sided.

If I've grossly misrepresented anyone in the pages of this book, I hope they will tell me so that I can apologize.

—Chad

Prologue

THE BALL BOUNCED OFF MY GLOVE and rolled all of the way to the fence.

I took off my hat—well, my helmet[1], actually—and slammed it into the ground.

The only good thing about the season was that it would soon be over. When it finally finished, I would never have to play baseball again.

I was twenty-two and sputtering to the end of a remarkably unsuccessful career as a college baseball player. I played at Whitman College, a small college in the southeast corner of Washington state. Four years of early mornings in the gym, late nights on the field, and long weekends on the road had amounted to a lot of time on the bench, watching the runs pile up on the opposing side of the scoreboard.

And it wasn't like I was dying to play, either. When I did get into the game, it was often to strike out or make an error. The only things keeping me on the field were my loyalty to my teammates and my grim determination to see things to the bitter end.

Rewind the clock a decade, however, and you would have encountered a very different ballplayer: a twelve-year-old rabid for baseball, probably fielding grounders or tweaking his stance in the backyard.

I started playing baseball when I was five years old. For over a decade, it was one of the most important things in my life. I slept with my glove under my pillow when I was trying to break it in. I wore grass-stains like badges of honor. I loved chalk, dedicated hours to curving the bill of my caps, and spent all winter dreaming of new batting gloves. For two or three years running, I was a Seattle Mariner for Halloween. I have clear memories of cautiously cursing God when it rained during the Little League season.

My friend Brian had a t-shirt: "Baseball is life," it said. "The rest is just details."

From age eight to eighteen, this was (a big part of) my philosophy, too.

By the end of college, however, everything had changed. Baseball had become a source of acute misery for me. What had been a life-long quest for the playoffs had ended in shipwreck. My teammates and I were drifting towards graduation and the merciful end, clinging to the splintered timbers of our childhood dreams.

If that sounds melodramatic, it's because it is—but that's how I felt.

How did it come to that? How did I go from dreaming of my next at-bat as an elementary schooler to hoping that my name wasn't even on the lineup card as a college senior?

Well, that's the story I will tell in this book.

Before I begin, however, there are a few questions to address. Why tell this story at all? Who wants to read about crushing failure and seemingly pointless misery? Wouldn't it be better, for me and for everyone else, to just file the experience away and move on?

After college, that's exactly what I wanted to do.

Baseball had been good to you for thirteen years, I reasoned with myself. *Isn't that enough? It's not like you were ever going to be a pro anyway. Why do you even care?*

I didn't know why I cared, but I did. Whitman baseball was stuck in my throat, and I needed to cough it out.

But how? I didn't know that either, so I just did what felt natural —tried to understand.

Even that project was unclear. Understand what? At first, I thought I needed to understand how we had played so poorly.

"Just how bad were you?" you might ask.

Well, from 2005 to 2008, our record was 21-126—which is a winning percentage of .167. If we had been a professional team, we would have had the second-worst winning percentage of all time. The only pro baseball team with a worse one was the 1899 Cleveland Spiders (.130). We gave up twenty runs or more eleven times, once giving up twenty-nine. In conference play, we were swept twenty-two times, including seven four-game sweeps in 2008.

So, we really sucked. I couldn't help wondering, How could we have been that bad?

Upon reflection, however, it became pretty obvious: We weren't that good. The other teams had better players, so—even if we did underperform—it's no surprise that they beat us easily.

The mystery wasn't why we had lost. The mystery, rather, was why the losing had affected me so much.

I mean, it was just baseball, right? We lost a lot of games, true, but off the field I was leading what many would consider a life of luxury on an Edenic college campus. Walk it off, tough guy, a reader might be tempted to say.

And I appreciate that logic. I even used it on myself. It seems there are some places that logic doesn't go, however.

For my younger self, baseball *hadn't* been just baseball; it had been life. My days as a college baseball player seemed to leave a stain on my entire baseball career—which meant they seemed to leave a stain on my life. Was there anything I could do to wipe it off?

As I tried, something many of my coaches had said kept coming back to me: "Baseball teaches you about life."

What, I wondered, *had baseball taught me about life—other than the fact that sometimes I'm not good enough to win?*

Hundreds of hours of reflection and dozens of revisions later, I know. It turns out that I didn't need to cough Whitman baseball out. I needed to swallow it whole, in order to digest the insights buried inside.

I can say that they were worth the heartburn.

So, pack up your gear and get on the bus, because we're about to go on a road trip. Along the way we'll pick up some excellent teammates, get hit with a variety of blunt objects, and find out what can happen if a person tries to stay in a story that is very much over. We'll be covered in dirt by the time the bus brings us home, but as my coaches also said, it's no fun to finish the game with a clean jersey anyway.

I.

—

EMERALDS AND DIAMONDS

It Isn't the Size of the Dog in the Fight

IN MY FIRST BASEBALL MEMORY, I am five years old.

I am standing in the parking lot of Briarcrest Elementary, playing with the foam bill of an orange hat as my dad takes bags of gear and buckets of balls from his car. A grass field opens up behind the portables, and there is something exciting to do there.

My dad was my first coach, and it was his job to teach fifteen five-year-olds how to play baseball. It was no small task, in part because baseball is a complicated sport. Imagine huddling up your five-year-olds and trying to explain the rules. It might take a little while to field all of the questions.

"What's a pitcher?"

"Where's the strike zone?"

"Why are they called runs and not points?"

"Can't we just play video games instead?"

Luckily, we didn't have to learn everything at once because we started with Tee-ball, not baseball. In Tee-ball, the pitcher doesn't need to throw the ball anywhere; it waits patiently on an adjustable rubber stand for someone to hit. All the five-year-olds have to do is swing.

They miss more often than you might expect, but eventually they hit it. Then all hell breaks loose. "Run!" parents yell, as the spongy ball dribbles towards the pitcher's mound. The children get excited and run.

Unfortunately, they only occasionally run in the right direction. "No, to first!" parents yell, maybe mortified but probably just having a good time.

But where is first? The children must think. Some run to first. Others skip straight to second, running past a bewildered pitcher. Still others go to third, perhaps assuming that the quickest way to score is to skip most of the bases.

It doesn't really matter where they run, because the defense may never get the ball to first base anyway. Throwing and catching are hard for adults; they're almost impossible for Tee-ballers. If I ever coach a Tee-ball team, I will tell my defenders to forego throwing entirely and just run the ball to first base. Because the batter will likely be running to the outfield fence, the fielder shouldn't have a tough time getting him or her out.

Getting outs is an important part of the game, after all. A half-inning doesn't end until the defense gets three. When none of the players can catch or throw, this becomes a problem.

Luckily, the planners of Tee-ball knew that, so they adapted the rules. A half-inning of Tee-ball ends not with three outs—which a team might never get—but when everyone has batted once. This rule change allows the games to flow much more smoothly than they otherwise would.

Even so, there's another obstacle for new players to hurdle. In addition to having confusing rules and skills that are hard to master, baseball can also be pretty boring. For long stretches of time, most of the players stand around doing nothing. Tee-ballers spend a lot of time playing with dirt, spinning in circles, and/or punching each other.

Why would anyone want to play this game? I understand that it sounds terrible, but for some reason I couldn't get enough of it. After a few weeks of practice, I started to understand what to do, and a rhythm emerged on the field. It wasn't baseball, but it resembled it. For the next thirteen years, all I wanted to do was get closer to the real thing.

Call to the Bullpen

After Tee-ball it was Little League. The tee disappeared, and the ball was handed to a pitcher, whose job it became to actually throw the ball towards the plate. Few pitchers could get it anywhere close, however, so after four balls a coach came out to pitch. Coaches generally had a tough time throwing strikes themselves, but players didn't get to walk, so coaches ended up striking out more than a few of their own players.

My dad continued to be my coach. He was an excellent coach. He was fair. He was encouraging. He umpired games when nobody else would. He defused parents who were about to blow up. I was lucky to have him.

It was his philosophy that the most talented guy doesn't always win. Hard work, he said, often trumps talent, and I was on board with that. Small as I was, that was pretty much my only hope.

It never bothered me that I was small, though. In elementary school, I didn't even think about it. My dad's philosophy certainly helped. The legendary season of the 1995 Seattle Mariners probably didn't hurt, either.

Reality Distorts Itself

In 1995, I was nine years old. Putty, perhaps, in the hands of the universe, receptive, to some extent, to the consequences of dumb luck. That year, the universe dealt Seattle baseball fans an improbably lucky hand. I watched in awe—and took mental notes —as the Mariners rose from the absolute dead.

Much has been written about the 1995 Seattle Mariners—in part because the franchise has done almost nothing since[2], but also because it was a nearly impossible season. The team was on the brink of being sold because their stadium, a lovable concrete abomination known as the Kingdome, was no longer deemed fit to house professional athletes. The ownership threatened to leave if funds couldn't be raised for a new ballpark.

The problem was that the Mariners were hopeless. They hadn't been to the playoffs in their nearly twenty-year history. Who wants to pay taxes to fund a sure loser? Somehow, the M's had to prove that they were worth the money. This win-or-go-bust background raised the stakes on the entire season.

It started poorly. In late May, the team lost Ken Griffey Jr., then a superstar at the top of his game, to injury. My dad and I were at the game. We cheered as he chased a fly ball towards the fence in right-center, leapt into the wall like Spider Man, and came down with the ball.

We then held our breath when he didn't get up.

On the ride back from the game, we learned that his wrist had been broken. My dad turned off the radio and sighed. "That's the end of the Mariners in Seattle," he said.

For a few months, the team didn't do anything to prove him wrong. In the middle of August, they were behind the then Cali - fornia Angels by thirteen games.

If a team is down by thirteen games in the middle of August, they are out of the race; teams don't come back from that far behind. When I was a kid, I didn't know that, however, because that year the Mariners did.

The Mariners have had their fair share of slogans over the years, from "You Gotta Love These Guys" to "Two Outs So What" to "True to the Blue." It all started in 1995 when their slogan was "Refuse to Lose."

The thing that made "Refuse to Lose" work was that the Angels simultaneously decided that they were going to *refuse to win*. Whereas the Mariners pulled out win after win, often in dramatic and improbable fashion, the Angels quietly and consistently choked. This pattern of the Mariners never losing and the Angels never winning played out faithfully for a month and a half. At the end of September, the two teams were tied. This meant they would play one game to decide who went to the playoffs.

For some reason the game was to be played at one o'clock on a weekday, and for some other reason my mom—always very committed to our education—let my brother and I leave school early to watch. We bounced up and down with glee on a gray leather couch as the Mariners destroyed the Angels 9-1.

That set us up for a playoff series—the first playoff series in Mariner history—against the Yankees. This, much like the regular season, didn't start well. The Mariners lost the first two games to go down 0-2. One more game and they would be out.

However, this was 1995, which meant that anything was possible. A few improbable victories later, the Mariners won the series 3-2. Griffey, having returned triumphantly from his early season injury, scored the decisive run in the 11th inning of game five on a double by Edgar Martinez. My family danced around in front of the TV, momentarily delirious in our excitement and disbelief.

The only way for the nine-year-old me to have gotten a more distorted view of reality would have been for the Mariners to go on to win the World Series with bench players after all of the starters had been abducted by aliens.

Of course, what actually happened was that they lost in the next round to the Cleveland Indians, but everything leading up to that point may have led my younger self to believe that anything was possible on a baseball field.

Baseball Players, Assemble

If I had enjoyed baseball before 1995, afterwards it became one of the main things in my life. It served a variety of purposes. In the spring, it was what filled my evenings. Rain or shine—more often rain—I put on my baseball pants and went to the fields. The diamond was my second home.

It was also where I made most of my friends. In elementary school, many boys played for the local Little League—North King County, in our case. Hamlin Park was where most of my friend - ships began and deepened.

The baseball didn't stop when the season was over. My friend Chris and I took batting lessons at Dave Henderson's Ballyard. My friend Kyle and I played hours of Super Baseball 2020 on Sega Genesis. Our family's backyard became a ballpark in miniature. My parents bought my brother and I big orange Wiffle ball bats and we took turns using them to bash plastic balls against the house. We invented an elaborate system of ground rules—off the house was live, on the roof was a homer, over the house was a *super cool* homer—and played whenever we could.

When my friends were busy, I took my glove and a ball into the backyard and played alone. I threw the ball against a screen and fielded it over and over again, calling my shots in my best Dave Niehaus[3] voice.

I don't know if it was fun or work, but it was what I wanted to do. Eventually, whatever it was paid off.

Refuse to Lose 2.0

I'm standing in front of an old shipping container at Hamlin Park. It's late May, the sun has yet to rise all of the way above the pine trees, and the air is probably still a little bit crisp. I run my finger down the sheet of paper tacked to the container—which houses the league's stock of uniforms—and nod when I see my name.

I made the twelve-year-old all-star team.

This was the summer of 1998, nearly three years after the Mariners' miraculous playoff run. That was just enough time for the impossible to have sunk into the unconscious of every young baseball player in the Seattle area. Underdogs everywhere (both self-styled and legitimate) now had a map they could use to chart a course from the deepest cellar to the postseason.

The North King County All-Stars pulled out that map and charted a course of our own. We were faithful to what was written on it. After a few weeks of practice, we lost the first game of the double-elimination tournament, putting us one loss away from the end of our season.

This might have been distressing, except for the fact that the Mariners had been in a similar situation a few years before. We all knew exactly what had happened then. Why couldn't it happen to us, too?

In the elimination game, we trotted out hawk-nosed, chicken-legged Tim Workman to keep us in the tournament. Tim was a fearsome force on a Little League mound. His fastball flew with actual precision and it came in hot. We pinned our season to his back and hoped he would carry us forward.

Tim pitched very well, but heading into the sixth and final inning, we were down by one. If we didn't score in the next at-bat, our season would be over.

Now three outs from victory, the other team—in my memory they are wearing red and blue uniforms—sends out their closer. A closer is a pitcher who comes into the game in the last inning in order to end it. Closers usually have a particularly effective pitch —a hard fastball, for example, or a slider that moves dramatically at the last instant. I don't know anything about this closer's pitches. I do know that he is six-foot-ten, two hundred and fifty pounds.

Or at least he looks it to me, measuring four-foot-nine, seventy-five pounds as I do. I watch this Goliath warm up through the green plastic slats threaded into the chain-link fence, knowing that my spot in the order is coming up.

The catcher throws down to second base and the inning begins. Somebody gets on base. Nick McEvoy goes out to pinch run. I watch from the on-deck circle as Owen Jacques successfully bunts him to second. I step into the batter's box, look up into the sky where the pitcher seems to stand, and wait.

I don't remember feeling confident. I don't remember feeling nervous. I just remember watching and waiting. Two pitches later, I hit a line drive over the second baseman's head. Nick McEvoy scores, and we end up winning the game. Red and blue goes home, but green and gold is still alive.

After the game, Tim's dad, Frank, looks at me with admiration. A long-time sports fan and devoted columnist for local papers, this is a man who appreciates a David and Goliath story.

"You know what, Frisky?" he says.

"What?" I ask.

"It isn't the size of the dog in the fight," he says.

I blink politely, waiting for him to continue.

"It's the size of the fight in the dog."

He smiles, eyes twinkling beneath bushy black eyebrows, then pats me on the shoulder and walks away. I stretch up a little bit taller, beaming as I turn to put away my gear.

We weren't done. In true Mariner fashion, we won at least one, maybe even two more games. Cameron Moffat threw a no-hitter. It was exhilarating to think that we might have a chance to win the tournament.

In even truer Mariner fashion, however, we lost in what I remember to be the semi-finals. I have no memories from that particular game. It must have been a boring loss.

Had we won, we would have been in the championship— against Woodinville Little League, a team that would end their season just one game away from the Little League World Series. They were on TV! I watched them!

They would have annihilated us, so maybe it's for the best that we didn't face them. It would have made it clear how far I, at least, was from ever really making it as a baseball player.

And what does it mean to "really make it" as a baseball player? Well, for the twelve-year-old me, it meant playing in the major leagues. It's absurd, but on some barely conscious level, that was my goal. I'd just had a game-winning hit in an all-star game. I wanted to believe that the sky was the limit.

While the dust of the tournament was still settling, I was already thinking about the next season. Little League was over, but baseball had just begun.

Sixty Feet, Six Inches

LITTLE LEAGUERS ARE SMALL PEOPLE, so it makes sense that they play on a small field. The bases are sixty feet apart. The mound is forty-six feet from home plate. This is good, because very few twelve-year-olds can throw a ball much farther than that.

But kids grow up. Eventually, they get too big for sixty-foot base paths and throw hard enough that nobody could ever hit anything thrown from forty-six feet away. At that point the lines expand. The distance between the bases grows to ninety feet, and the mound gets pushed back to sixty feet, six inches.

At first, almost nobody in my league was ready for it. I certainly wasn't. To a thirteen-year-old on his first day out of Little League, the infield felt oceanic. The bases were white buoys anchored in an endless sea of dirt. The extra thirty feet to first base felt like a mile. Most of us plowed through it like tugboats through chop, huffing and puffing and nearly dead by the time we reached the base.

It was even worse for the fielders. The distance between bases increased by thirty feet per base, but the infield is a box that grows on all sides, so the distance the fielders had to throw increased a lot more than the distance batters had to run.

For at least a year, getting on base became very easy. All you had to do was hit the ball on the ground and run. Unless you happened to move like a manatee, you would almost never be thrown out. The field was just too big for most thirteen-year-old bodies.

I loved the change. Moving to the bigger field felt like a rite of passage. It involved literally moving up, because the new fields were up a tall, leafy hill from the fields we'd used as Little Leaguers. The fact that my dad wasn't my coach[4] added to the effect. I was on my own in a new league, and my new team was, believe it or not, the Mariners.

The real Mariners were pretty good at the time. They had Ken Griffey Jr., Edgar Martinez, Jay Buhner, Randy Johnson, and a young Alex Rodriguez. Our Mariners weren't too shabby, either. We had the Little League home-run king, Mike Burgher. We had eye-black smearing, doubles-bashing, already-bearded Brian Perry. We had teal uniforms and the most hard-nosed coach in the league, Brian's older brother, Paul. We also had me, the little hustling enigma, still glowing from his all-star exploits the summer before.

We played well. At least in my memory, Mike hit the ball hard and struck people out, Brian hit doubles and frightened people with his eye-black, and I ran as fast as I could from the dugout to my position. Everything was right with the world.

Lightning Strikes

But then it happened. I got my first baseball-related injury. It wouldn't be the last or the worst—which is saying something, because I was about to get hit in the mouth with a bat.

We are standing around before a game, waiting for an umpire to arrive. Half of the team is clustered together, talking smack about their math teachers or ranking the seventh-grade girls for attractiveness. One of the guys has a bat and is casually swinging it. The blue and black stick of aluminum draws lines in the spring air. I am off to the side. Suddenly everybody starts laughing, so I decide that I want to join the conversation and casually wander over. At just that moment, my teammate swings.

It is my fault. I should have announced my presence, and I shouldn't have walked up behind someone holding a bat. But I did, and the backswing catches me right in the mouth.

Luckily, it isn't the front swing. Luckily, my teammate isn't swinging hard. Even a casual backswing, however, is enough to draw blood. It flows through my fingers and onto my teal jersey. My head fills with a swarm of frightened bumblebees, and I run into the dugout, screaming. Not because it hurts—I clearly remember a sensation of high-frequency vibration without any pain—but because I think someone needs to know what has happened.

Hours later, I squint into a bathroom mirror. A large "V" is missing from the middle of my front teeth. I look like a vampire drawn by a four-year-old. I want to explore the gap with my tongue but can't because at least one nerve is exposed.

After that, I become good friends with my dentist. I get a root canal. The smell of my teeth being ground down reminds me of old fish. I go back a week later, and the dentist fills the V-shaped gap with putty. I no longer look like a poorly imagined vampire. I run my tongue against the lumps of high-end Play-Doh globbed onto the back of my teeth and feel instead like a low-end cyborg.

Rule-Book Thumping

The injury didn't keep me out of the lineup for long; it was time for the playoffs, and I needed to be on the field. In the semi-final game, Mike was king. In the first inning, he sent a sixty-five mph fastball through descending twilight and into the trees for a homer. He also pitched, grinding the other team into dust with fastballs of his own. We were headed to the championship, which was just a few days away.

Mike was our best pitcher. After the semi-final game, he and his dad were talking with the coach about how to ice his arm. But I—obsessed with adhering to every rule ever invented—was concerned. Normally reserved, I felt no choice but to point out when I thought a rule was being violated.

"If Mike pitches," I said, half-strident, half-petrified, "won't we be disqualified?"

They stopped talking and looked at me. Mike looked annoyed. I don't blame him, but he couldn't legally pitch in the championship game because players in our league weren't allowed to pitch in back-to-back games. The coach thought about it for a second and then nodded. "He's right," he said.

And now for my ulterior motive: While I *was* concerned about rules, I also wanted to pitch, and after Mike I must have been next in line. Coach Perry gave me the nod, and that's how I weaseled my way onto the mound for the championship game.

The night before the game, I went to the field with my dad. He squatted behind the plate and held up a floppy brown catcher's mitt that he must have had since the 70s. I toed the rubber and tried to make it pop. I only threw fifty mph, so the best I could manage was a polite *whap*.

That'll have to be enough, I thought.

Torpedoed

I kick at the dirt around the pitcher's rubber with my black plastic cleats, more to kill time than anything else. I look over at the gray jersey standing on third base. There is one on second and another on first. It's the fifth inning of seven. The game is close, and I want to keep it that way.

I don't have any particularly effective pitches. My curveball doesn't do anything, my fastball is slow, and I don't know how to throw a changeup (a pitch that is supposed to look like a fastball while actually being much slower). What I do have is a particularly *strange* pitch. I don't know where I got the idea for it—I have enough difficulty throwing strikes normally—but at some point in the season, I had developed a submarine pitch.

If you're reading this book, my assumption is that you know how a pitcher usually throws. The ball comes at the batter from somewhere above the pitcher's shoulder. A sidearm pitch is thrown with the arm more or less parallel to the ground. A submarine pitch comes from even lower. If sidearm represents the water-line, a submarine pitch appears to come at the batter from underwater. There are a few submariners in the major leagues. They wind up normally and then dip down, whipping their arm in a "C" that resembles a softball pitcher's. Good submariners appear to release the ball from just above the dirt.

I am not a good submariner, but no other thirteen-year-old throws a submarine pitch, so the sheer unexpectedness of it is enough to make some people swing and miss. It has worked all day, but it has been mostly luck.

I step off the mound, remove my hat, and wipe the sweat from my forehead, trying not to think about Ben Winslow. Ben Winslow is the Frank Thomas of our league. He is huge. He plays first base. He hits the ball really hard. With the bases loaded in the 5th inning, he steps into the batter's box.

I look in for the sign. One is fastball, two is whatever excuse I have for a curveball, three is submarine. The catcher puts down a three. I take a breath, wind up, and throw.

Ben takes a huge swing, nearly drilling himself into the ground. The ball hits the catcher's mitt with a polite *whap*. Strike one. I can feel the sweat against my hatband. It is slimy with fear.

Ben snorts like an angry bull and digs his feet into the batter's box. I look in for the sign. Two fingers. I grip the ball like I think I am supposed to, crisp red seams digging into the side of my middle finger, and throw.

The ball sails high into the air, arcing towards home plate in a lazy parabola. There is no snap on it, no point at which it breaks any more noticeably than any other. But somehow Ben misses it. The lazy line terminates in the catcher's mitt for strike two.

The catcher throws the ball back to me and for a minute I think we might get out of the inning. I return to the rubber and look in for the sign. The catcher puts down three fingers.

Why is coach calling for another submarine pitch? Ben clearly wasn't fooled by the first one. *Oh well*, I think, *he's the adult*, and come set.

I wind up, my arm dropping down near the dirt before flicking towards home plate. The ball leaves my hand and I watch in horror as it glides gently into the middle of the strike zone. Ben's eyes light up and he takes a swing. This time he doesn't miss. I spin and watch the ball zip down the left-field line. All of the runners score and Ben eases into second for a double.

That's how I got the loss in the championship game. To his credit, Mike never mentioned it.

All Aboard

The next year, I was one of the top draft picks in the league.

At least, that was the rumor. I don't know if it was true. What I do know is that I was drafted to the worst team I had ever played for (at the time). We were the Pirates. Our uniforms were black nylon, our socks were mustard yellow, and our record was abysmal.

But I loved that team. One reason was that I thought I had been picked highly. That was an ego boost. The person who had picked me was a new coach—not my dad, and not Coach Perry. I unfortunately don't remember his name, but I do remember that he was fun to play for.

That was probably because I got to play wherever I wanted. I played catcher. I pitched a lot. The amplitude on my curveball rose in time with my ego, at its zenith soaring above the backstop before plummeting into the catcher's mitt. It still didn't break. The only force operating upon it was gravity. But some people couldn't hit it, so I felt pretty good about myself.

And if we didn't win a lot of games? Well, it wasn't the end of the world. On the one hand, I personally played well. (It is selfish to care more about your own batting average/ERA than your team's record, but, oh well, I did.)

On the other hand, I knew that my baseball career was far from over. It was eighth grade and in a few short months, high school would begin.

As far as I was concerned, that was the big show.

II.

—

GREEN AND GOLD

The Next Hill

SHORECREST HIGH SCHOOL—home of the Scots—was (and still is) right down the hill from Hamlin 5 and 6. The school's baseball field was perched atop another hill on the other side of the school. It was my dream to climb to the top and take my place on the varsity team.

That would have to wait for a few years, however. First, I had to prove myself on the C-team. Our lineup was a reprise of many familiar characters, most of whom I had been playing with and against since elementary school. In four years, would we be able to come together on the varsity team to take home a state cham - pionship?

That was the dream. In early March, I returned to Hamlin 6, where the C-Team played, and got to work.

The Stoic in High Socks

Moving to the C-Team meant meeting a new coach. We had three of them, in fact. Each one had a personal stake in our improvement. There was Troy Griffith, the friendly older brother of our first baseman. There was Mike Collins, the bearded older brother of our shortstop. And then there was Frank Workman.

You may remember Frank as Tim's dad. He had known all of us for a long time. He knew our batting stances, our throwing motions, and whether or not we hustled.

He was also my first Philosopher Coach. His brand of philosophy was earthy, and his primary theme was personal accountability. "Excuses are like assholes," he told us one day. "Everybody has one and they all stink."

We were a group of freshmen who had just recently crawled out of junior high school. Someone probably laughed—either nervously or cynically—when he said it. But Frank was serious.

"It's not whether you win or lose, fellas, but how you play the game."

The lessons started with how we played catch. At the beginning of every practice or before every game, teams generally stretch, line up down one foul line, and warm up their arms. Almost immediately, balls begin flying over people's heads. This usually means one person runs to chase the ball while the other one stands there.

To Frank, this didn't make much sense. Why should the person who made a bad throw just stand there while his partner—who most likely did nothing wrong—chases the ball? His solution was simple and elegant.

"If you overthrow your partner, you run as much as he does."

People looked at him with a mixture of disbelief and annoyance, but he was, again, serious. After every overthrow, two players ran. It's not clear whether or not this reduced the number of bad throws, but it probably helped us get fit.

One of Frank's superpowers was the ability to see through bullshit. At the end of one practice, he gave us homework. We were supposed to look up the history of some baseball stadium.

The next day as we were playing catch, he asked one of the play - ers if he had done it.

Nobody had done it. The poor boy he called upon sputtered, trying to find a way out.

"I was going to, but—" he said.

Frank cut him off. "No, you weren't," he said.

The boy looked at him, still sputtering.

"Let me tell you something," he said. "You'll remember this your whole life. Anything that comes after 'I was going to, but' is an excuse."

He paused. The bill of his cap shaded his eyes, but his smile sparkled in the sun. "And you know how I feel about excuses."

One day, we were locked in a close game. With runners on and two outs in a late inning, the other team hit a ground ball to our shortstop, AJ. It bounded across the craggy infield, and I watched from second base as AJ scooped it up and threw to first. I watched the ball approach the first baseman's glove, and then I watched it bounce off the first baseman's glove and hit the ground. A run scored, and we eventually lost.

"Throw the ball, catch the ball," Frank said the next day at practice.

We were warming up. He shook his head in despair as players ran into the outfield to retrieve overthrows, throwing partners chasing after them.

"It's a simple game, boys," he called out. "Throw the ball, catch the ball."

When we had finished, he looked at the first baseman from the day before. "If you practice catching the ball now, you won't drop it in a game."

The first baseman's face went red. "I didn't drop it," he said.

Frank raised an eyebrow.

The fourteen-year-old repeated himself. "I didn't drop it," he said, indignant. "I just didn't catch it."

I thought Frank was going to have a seizure.

Frank did more than just hold us accountable for our mistakes. He also attempted to remind us of our successes. One rainy day, he elected to have practice in a classroom rather than send us home. We sat at tables, facing the front of the room.

"What is your clearest baseball memory?" Frank asked.

I blinked. The game-winning hit in the all-star game was—I think—the first thing that came to mind. When it was my turn to speak, however, something else came out of my mouth.

"One time in Little League," I said, "I hit an in-the-park home-run, but Drew's dad called me out."

This did happen, and it was a bitter memory. I was probably eight. It was a typically Pacific Northwest spring day: cold, gray, and wet. I got a pitch to hit and actually hit it so well that I sent the outfielders scurrying back to chase it. I raced around the bases, rounded third, and touched home plate before the ball made it back to the infield.

It was my first home run. The exultation was profound, but very short-lived. Before I knew it, the umpire had his fist in the air and was calling me out.

What? I thought in disbelief. The other team said I had missed third base and appealed to the ump. He agreed. I was devastated. *I touched it with the outside of my foot!* And I did, I think. At any rate, I was out and wouldn't hit another home run until my senior year of college.

Frank looked at me quizzically, black eyebrows bunching up.

"Are you sure that's your most memorable moment, Frisky?"

It wasn't, but I didn't want to show off. Or maybe I was afraid of being mocked for saying something honest. Whatever my moti -

vation, I remember shrugging and letting the conversation move on.

All Said and Done

When the dust settled, we had lost more games than we'd won. It wasn't a terrible season, but it wasn't a season that marked us as future state championship contenders, either. I remember feeling disappointed with our play, but still optimistic. We had three years to improve, I figured. We'd be ready when the time came.

The letters Coach Collins passed out at the end of the year were a big part of that optimism. They were written in blue ink on yellow legal paper and impressed with his sincere encourage - ment. During the season we'd had some practices with the JV and varsity players. The other coaches, seeing that I didn't have a textbook swing, tried to teach me how to hit with more power:

"Load your hands this way."

"Use your front side like this."

"Put more of your back leg into it."

I tried to listen, but I didn't understand what they were asking me to do. My swing fell apart. Coach Collins saw that.

"Don't let anyone mess with your swing," he wrote. "Play the game the way you play it. That's more than enough."

It felt good to be seen for who I was—a singles hitter who left it all on the field. With his encouragement, I turned towards the next season.

JV

SOPHOMORE YEAR I MOVED from the C-Team to JV. Joining the JV team meant new jerseys, new hats, and a new field. I left Hamlin for good, finally making the journey to the Shorecrest field. In my sixteen-year-old eyes, it sparkled like a gem. It was surrounded by evergreens, flanked by green dugouts, and covered with green grass, so walking up to it felt like finding a secret garden. I opened the gate and hustled to the dugout, certain that the winning would start soon.

To help us on our journey, we had two new coaches: Puetz and Steve. Up until that point, I had related to coaches with the reverence and fear of a small child. For the most part, I did whatever they told me to do without even thinking about it. This year, however, my eyes began to open to the possibility that my coaches weren't gods but well-intentioned, fallible middle-aged men.

What first got me thinking were the pet phrases. Puetz had one. I heard it so often that I started to wonder. *Does everyone really need the exact same advice?* It suddenly occurred to me that Puetz wasn't the only coach with a pet phrase. *All* of my coaches had had at least one.

"See the ball, hit the ball," they said.

"Strong frontside."

"Squash the bug."

"Knob first."

"Box it up."

"Let it travel."

"Throw your hands."

"Load and explode."

What does any of that mean? Even after many years of playing baseball, I only understand some of it. Having been a high school tennis coach for a few years, I appreciate that sometimes a coach just has to say *something*. The coach may even have a clear point. Whether or not that message makes it to the players, however, is another story.

Puetz's particular pet phrase was "pop the hips." He would stand outside the batting cage and watch a player take a few swings. After a moment he would hold up a hand, tell the pitcher to wait, and then duck under the netting.

"Your swing looks good," he would say. "But you've got to remember to pop the hips." Then he would pantomime some - thing that was supposedly popping his hips. It looked more like a 1970s dance move than anything else[5]. When I tried to do it, I realized that I had no idea what he was talking about. He nodded enthusiastically, which is probably the best a coach in his posi - tion can do.

"That's right, pop the hips, just like that!"

Ultimately, I had to content myself with squashing the bug. I was relatively confident that I knew how to do that.

Roadblocks

I had hoped this would be the year that we made great strides as a team. A story had been playing in my mind since the first day of high school. We were a group of rising stars, unknown by the media but destined for great things. We would, through hard work and dedication, improve day by day and battle our way into the state tournament.

You might recognize this as the story of 1995 Mariners. It was also the story of our twelve-year-old all-star team. It was how I understood my place on the baseball field. Our mediocre fresh - man season hadn't done much to disrupt that story. I figured that we were just a little bit slow getting started.

Unfortunately, sophomore year we didn't show any signs of picking up steam. As soon as the season began, we started to get pummeled. The sense of possibility that animates the beginning of every season stagnated, quickly turning into frustration and then disinterest. This is a feeling I later became very familiar with, but at the time it was new and upsetting. I simmered on low heat and did nothing.

Puetz and Steve eventually boiled over. After one particularly lackluster loss, Puetz gathered us behind the third-base dugout and let us have it. He said the things baseball coaches must say when they're angry—something about respecting the game, something about taking pride in your work, something about horseshit.

Then it was Steve's turn.

Let me say that we were not nice to Steve—actually, we were cruel to Steve. He was a volunteer, who didn't even have a son on the team. He came out every day and hit us grounders, which was very generous of him. Unfortunately, he was pretty bad at hitting grounders, so we mocked him behind his back.

Another time, it was raining so we practiced in the gym. Two of the guys started throwing Lite-Flites (practice balls made of solid yellow foam) at each other. One of them sailed past its intended target and nailed Steve right in the testicles. He was down on the ground for an uncomfortably long time. After that, all anyone needed to do to get a laugh out of the team was make a reference to Lite-Flites.

Two years later, we went go-karting for a team-bonding trip. Everyone named their kart at the sign-in desk. One person chose "Die Steve"[6].

After Puetz finished his tirade, he turned to Steve.

"Got anything, Steve?"

Steve, tragically, had something. He stepped forward, bristling with emotion, perhaps pent-up from all of the weeks of mistreatment we had subjected him to up to that point.

"How could you let those yahoos come in here and beat you like that?"

He pronounced it *yay-hoos*, and we had to fight to keep from cracking up. Some people didn't fight very hard.

"I'm so angry that I could…"

He paused for a moment, contemplating the appropriate way to express his frustration. He probably should have shut it down right there. He probably should have shrugged his shoulders, suggesting that our attitudes were so poor as to defy description. At worst, he should have turned around and stormed off. But he was already in the windup, which meant that he had to throw the pitch.

"I'm so angry that I could kick a rock!" He said, punctuating it with a snort. Then I think he actually kicked a rock.

We were losing it. Even I was losing it, and I had an almost pathological fear of upsetting authority figures. Puetz stormed away and pledged not to return until we had our shit together.

He was getting paid and so couldn't stay away for very long. Ultimately, he missed about half of a practice. That said, even that short of an absence made it clear to me that something wasn't right.

Motivational Speaking Is Hard

What, exactly, was wrong with us? Maybe we just weren't good —but maybe we were lazy. I deeply wanted it to be laziness. It's hard to do anything about lack of ability, but lack of effort may be fixable. I was a co-captain of the team and decided to address what I wanted the problem to be.

In the huddle at a joint JV/varsity practice, I announced that the next day I would have something to say. One of the varsity guys patted me on the back. I was too busy peeing myself to feel very encouraged.

Even though I had played baseball with those guys my whole life, I was intimidated by many of them. But I was also co-captain, for some reason, and so felt like I had to say something. I ended up writing a speech and then spent at least forty-five minutes rehearsing it in the shower.

Before practice the next day, I gathered the team together. "Guys," I said, the script unfurling itself in front of my eyes as if on a teleprompter, "Something is wrong."

I then gave a bad speech. It was long. It was overly emotional and clearly rehearsed. It didn't match my personality or my relationship to the other guys on the team. I think they nodded their heads dutifully and then ran out to their positions. Later, two of them came over to me. They had big smiles on their faces.

"Did you memorize that speech?" They asked.

"No," I lied, and then ran away.

The season ended without much change in our play. I had played well, so towards the end of the season, I got called up to varsity. My eyes sparkled as I stepped onto the bus—and then sat a very deferential distance from everybody else. At the game, the senior second baseman took me under his wing.

"That's going to be you out there," he said. We were batting, and he was pointing to the second base area. "It'll be your team." I nodded fiercely, ready to do my part to lead us to victory.

I was in math class with one of the players on the varsity team. His name was Derek, and he was a year older than me. He heard that I had batted .400 that year.

"Is that good?" A reader might be wondering. In baseball, a .300 batting average is considered very good. A .400 batting average is almost mythical. The last player to manage one in the major leagues was a man named Ted Williams, who accom-plished it in 1941. The high school season is much shorter than a professional season and the competition isn't quite as intense, so .400 averages are somewhat more common. My own .400 aver-age was inflated by bloopers to right field and dinky groundballs that found holes, but the number still carries a lot of magic.

Derek wrote in my yearbook: "Can't wait to have that batting average on varsity next year." I glowed but didn't think twice about whether or not I could deliver.

Summer Ball

At the end of the school year, I was invited to play for the Shoreline summer league team. It was coached by the Shorecrest varsity coach and was made up of players from Shorecrest—my school—and our cross-town rival, Shorewood. It felt like a tune-up for the real deal.

Unfortunately, we broke down pretty quickly. One particularly hot Saturday captures the spirit of the season. We were playing a double header at the dust bowl of Roosevelt High School. We lost the first game handily and were getting throttled in the second.

Our coach came back to the dugout after an unimpressive at-bat and found us eating popsicles that somebody's mom had slipped through the fence. I don't remember whether or not he waited for the game to end before making us run.

That season might have been the thing to finally shake my faith in the story I thought I was living in, but I found plenty of reasons to keep it in place.

It was just summer ball, nobody was serious. And besides, our best players were on other teams anyway.

Another reason I didn't worry too much about the future was that I had made a new friend, Clete. Clete showed up to summer ball with a green and yellow canvas bag, a TPX bat, and a char- acteristically goofy smile. He didn't go to Shorecrest at the time, but he was scheduled to transfer in the following year. He was good, so with him added to the lineup, I figured that junior year would be something special.

Unfortunately, things didn't go according to my plans.

Junior Year

FOR MANY HIGH SCHOOL STUDENTS, junior year is the most intense. The prospect of college looms for those who plan to apply. SAT prep begins, AP classes multiply, and romantic relationships begin and blow up. These things were not unimportant to me. None of them, however, were enough to crowd out baseball.

We took our preparation seriously. The winter before the season started, the whole team went to a local batting cage for hitting lessons. We met a coach with his own set of magic words ("Top half!"). I got pretty decent at hitting the ball on what appeared to be a line, but only while hitting off a tee with my back foot planted in the middle of a tire.

Frank, at that point a regular volunteer for the team, came up to me.

"Swing's looking pretty good, Frisky," he said.

I shrugged. Hitting well off a tee was one thing. I wondered what would happen when I faced an actual pitcher.

"Thanks," I said. "But will it translate?"

Spring Cleaning

February came. The season was only a few weeks away, and we had a job to do: make our field playable.

The Shorecrest baseball field was notoriously terrible. The fact that it had appeared so beautiful the year before was more about what it meant to me than what it looked like. At the time, it had a lumpy grass infield with small dirt cutouts around the bases. The warning track was mostly weeds, and the pitcher's mound was a constant mudslide that refused to retain any shape. As a team, we dedicated a month of Saturdays before the season to making it resemble an actual baseball field.

I'm not sure how we got the responsibility, but Clete and I found ourselves in charge of the Gator. The Gator was a green and yellow John-Deere service vehicle. We loaded it with dirt from a pile of clay outside the fence and drove it to the bases. We loaded it with trash from the dugouts and drove it to the dump - sters behind the school. We spent a fair amount of time joyriding in the parking lot, jumping speed bumps at ten miles per hour.

Riding back and forth between the dumpster and the field, we invented a game that had no name but could be called "Laugh Until It Gets Funny." This game involved fake laughing in an idiotic way until the stupidity of the exercise triggered genuine laughter. It worked surprisingly well.

It's good that we invented it, because as soon as the season started, I would need a laugh.

The Big Show

By March, the field was as good as we could make it. Clete and I both made varsity. It seemed as if all of the baseball I had ever played had been training for this moment.

Much to my surprise, however, I found myself on the bench.

I hadn't sat on the bench since Little League, and that was tolerable because my dad had made everybody sit on the bench. Being on the bench didn't necessarily mean a boy wasn't good enough to play. It was just a part of being on the team. Now, however, sitting on the bench seemed to mean exactly that.

It brought back a memory I hadn't relived in a while. When I was thirteen, I tried out for a select team. It was filled with many of the Woodinville stars who had nearly made it to the Little League World Series the summer before. Tim was on the team. Matt Tuiasosopo, future Mariner, was on the team. Mike, future D-1 player, tried out. I felt outclassed in a way I never had before.

The other guys were big. They were fast. They hit the ball really hard. I didn't even know I was allowed to move my feet when playing catch. During warm-ups, I stood rooted in one place, reaching out for what struck me as errant throws from my part - ner. The coach looked at me with exasperation—"Go get the ball!" he said.

I was indignant. *What do you mean, go get the ball? Why aren't you telling the other guy to throw it to me?*

Clearly, I was wrong. While playing catch, you should move to get the ball if you need to. It's a pretty basic thing, so no wonder the coach was annoyed that I wasn't doing it. After getting home I immediately jettisoned the experience and then went to Hamlin 5 to strike out a few normal kids with curveballs that looked like rainbows.

My first year on varsity, those feelings of inadequacy came back with a vengeance. They didn't feel quite right, though. The Woodinville guys were clearly a class or two or ten beyond me. But the Shorecrest guys? Was I really not good enough to play with them?

Memories of a .400 batting average and game-winning hits floated through my mind as I rode the pine and somewhat bitterly watched my friends play.

Attitude and Hustle

The coach of the varsity team was a man named Medalia. He had a mustache, always wore a green pullover, and had a very clear motto: "There are only two things under your control: attitude and hustle." This made me feel good, because attitude and hustle were all I had.

Well, to be fair, I had hustle. My attitude came and went.

When I started junior year on the bench, there was a part of me that thought it was somebody else's fault. *Medalia must think I'm too small*, I thought. *Puetz must have forgotten to tell him how good I am.*

After a certain point, however, those thoughts started to smell like excuses, and excuses never smelt the same after Frank. I had to consider the possibility that I wasn't playing because I wasn't good enough. I decided that my only choice was to work harder.

I had always been good at working hard. Despite the fact that I met many of my friends there, the baseball field wasn't just a place to hang out. You might say that it wasn't *even* a place to hang out. It was where I went to work.

There was a flaw in my work ethic, however. Much of my energy went into skill building, but some of it was simply signaling to my coach (and teammates) that I was trying.

Junior year I went through a phase where I tripped and fell running to first base a lot. I'd hit a weak ground ball to shortstop and then put all of my frustration into sprinting down the first-base line. At that time, I moved pretty decently, but it's hard to beat out a groundball to short.

After getting down the line as fast as I could, I would inevitably be out by a couple of steps—clearly out, but close enough to pretend that I wasn't. I would hit the bag and collapse, as if I had exerted the last ounce of my strength heroically reaching for it.

I did my best guys, that fall said. Plus, *pity me a little.*

The thing that made all of those theatrics possible, however, was some effort that had paid off. Before that year, I had never been fast enough to make any play close. Something had happened in fall practice to change that.

Keeping Me on My Toes

On the baseball field, it's not uncommon for people—myself included—to think that small guys will be fast. Are small guys fast? They're usually faster than three-hundred pounders, I suppose, but the fastest guys tend to be tall and muscular. Personally, though I was relatively small, before my junior year I was not fast.

Again, it wasn't because I wasn't trying. I ran the same way I did everything else on a baseball field: with five-hundred percent effort. The only problem was that I thought the best way to use that effort was by stomping. If I had weighed more than a hundred pounds, I probably would have caused an earthquake.

There were a lot of really fast guys on the team my junior year. Mike was fast. Derek was fast. Brian Jackson was fast. In an unexpected turn of events, I was about to join their ranks.

On a cold fall night at Shoreline Stadium, we lined up to do sprints. Before we started, Coach Medalia gave us a tip about form.

"Dig your toes into the ground," he said, "and pump your arms like this."

He pistoned his arms forward and backwards, keeping his elbows close to his sides. A bolt of lightning went through me. I didn't know I was allowed to run like that! I thought I was

41

supposed to slam the entire surface of my feet into the ground and to swing my arms around like a discus thrower.

I made the tweaks, and suddenly I was fast. Not as fast as Mike, not as fast as Derek, but much faster than I had ever been. I was shocked and pleased. During the season, I beat out a couple of infield hits (and pratfell into a half-dozen heaps after mildly close plays). I didn't get into the game as often as I was used to but learning how to run gave me a chance.

I don't remember how the season turned out. Did we make the playoffs? If so, we must not have won very many games. Whatever happened, my newfound speed gave me a reason to look forward to the next year—my senior season.

You might not be surprised to learn that my optimism remained intact. Sure, we hadn't been great freshman or sophomore year. Sure, summer league had been embarrassing, and I had spent a fair amount of junior year on the bench. Hope, however, springs eternal on the baseball field, and I thought the next year would be the best year I'd ever had.

Surprisingly, that wasn't far from the truth.

State Bound?

SENIOR YEAR FELT LIKE the culmination of all things. Seven years of elementary school, two years of middle school, three years of high school. All of the work put into them results in a flowering of some sort. This was the year we would blossom, shine, catch fire, and go all of the way to the state tournament. That, at least, was the hope.

Let's Go

Our time was short, and Medalia didn't waste any of it. As the season approached, we woke up early. Practice started at six in the morning. I rolled out of bed only barely alive—once backing directly into my mom's mini-van on the way to practice—and made it to the gym, where Medalia waited with a stopwatch.

Afternoon practice was equally serious. I remember throwing my bat bag over the fence and climbing over because there was no other way to get in. I remember picking up my bag and running into the dugout because we had to.

There was a big reason that things felt more intense that year. Coach Medalia had gained an assistant: Woodward[7].

A Man Among Boys

Woodward came on as assistant coach at the beginning of the year. In retrospect, I feel for him. Gaining the trust of a group of eighteen-year-old boys is no easy task. They are territorial. They think they know everything. If you try to assert authority over them without first earning their respect, they will make your life a living hell. I think we probably made Woodward's life a living hell.

He was most likely in his mid-to-late twenties and had played baseball in college, so I assume that he was a good player. He probably wanted to help us become good players, too, by working hard and taking baseball seriously. Unfortunately, we weren't quite ready for that.

During winter workouts, we were doing ab exercises. Apparently, some people were slacking off. "If you're going to half-ass these," Woodward said suddenly, "then you might as well not do them." I nodded and tried harder, but I was a teacher's pet.

I wasn't immune to the wrath of Woodward, however.

It was a Saturday morning in early spring. A group of Little Leaguers had come to the field to visit us. We were supposed to be running a hitting clinic, but it felt like a huge waste of time. The boys didn't listen to us and their dads didn't even notice we were there.

"Maybe if you tried..." I said to one boy, venturing some advice (which, to be fair, was probably not very good anyway). His dad put another ball on the tee and told him to swing before I had even finished.

Well, this sucks, I thought. Nobody enjoys giving up their Saturday morning to be ignored by elementary schoolers and their dads, especially not eighteen-year-olds. I made no effort to hide my displeasure. Woodward read my body language and inter-preted it in his own way.

He came up behind me. "Hey," he said, putting a hand on my shoulder.

I turned to him. He wasn't smiling.

"I don't care how many beers you had last night," he said, "you need to suck it up for these kids."

That upset me in a way that only a falsely accused teenager can be upset. At the time, I was petrified by the mere thought of alcohol. I hadn't been to a party since sixth grade. I don't think I'd even been in the presence of an open beer can, unless it was held by one of my parents.

"I stayed up until ten-thirty playing The Legend of Zelda," I snapped. "And none of these kids could care less about us."

Then I walked away.

Mutiny

With two such strong personalities at the helm, some form of pushback was inevitable. It came in a variety of forms. I remem-ber blurting out something in the locker room one day before practice.

"It's like the coaches are on a cliff looking down on us," I said, riding some form of inspiration that I hadn't been in contact with two years previously, "and they don't hear anything we say." I remember a reflective silence following, and nobody asked me if I had memorized anything.

Another day, someone came in from the outfield complaining about always being "chastised" by the coaches. Woodward followed close behind, chastising.

The most entertaining mutineer, however, was Clete. He couldn't say much to the head coach if he wanted to stay in the lineup, so he contented himself with the occasional jab behind his back. Woodward was a different story. Clete made it his mission to get under Woodward's skin, and he was good at it.

The Voice

The thing that bothered Woodward the most was probably the Voice. The Voice was a very strange mode of communication that Clete shared with a guy on the team named Luke, better known as Boranger. Boranger was a gentle giant who would have been a very solid contributor if he hadn't gotten his hand smashed between two football helmets in the fall of our junior year. By senior year, he was my second-closest friend on the team.

That said, the Voice was off-limits even to me. It was something special between Clete and Boranger. The Voice was alternately hilarious and irritating. If a giant tree sloth could speak English and did so with a jar of molasses in its mouth, then it would speak in the Voice. Sentences spoken in the Voice were very short, typically consisting of a single word. "Hey" and "Whoa" were the most common.

I think Woodward hated the Voice. It's not hard to see why. It was kind of annoying and probably fed right into what I assume was his mostly accurate perception of us as total screw-offs. Clete knew that. He would one day use it to push Woodward over the edge.

It happened during a particularly lackluster practice. After enduring our poor effort for some time, Medalia had seen enough. "Lock it up!" He yelled, his way of calling us into a huddle. We hustled towards the third base dugout. While we waited for him to arrive, Clete and Boranger started conversing in the Voice.

"Hey," said Boranger.

"Whoa," replied Clete.

Nobody knew what the hell they were talking about, but everybody knew to leave them alone. Everybody, that is, except Woodward. He couldn't help making a jab. Clete parried. At that point, Medalia arrived and was ready to speak.

But Woodward wasn't finished. Much like Steve a few years earlier, he should have just let it go, but couldn't. The Voice was in his head, gumming up the works. He sneered and said something in a mockery of the Voice just as Medalia started to talk. Medalia glared daggers at Woodward. Woodward glared daggers at Clete. Clete just laughed. Then we ran for a long time.

It was all fun and games that day, but eventually Clete would pay.

Move Your Feet

Clete was one of our shortstops. He was a very reliable fielder, and I trusted his burnt orange, professionally pancaked Wilson A2000 with every ball that came at it.

And yet, as far as Coach Medalia was concerned, Clete had cement in his shoes. "Move your feet, Clete!" He would say after almost every ground ball that was hit to him. Did Clete, in fact, need to move his feet? It's hard to say. I always thought they moved as much as anyone else's. But after every ground ball in practice, Medalia would grimace, regrip his fungo, and yell, "Goddammit, Clete, move your feet!"

Perhaps this was an attempt to remind Clete who was boss. Halfway through the season, Clete got the message. "Move your feet, Clete!" Medalia yelled and tossed a ball towards the gray, cloudy sky. As far as I could tell, Clete did, fielding the ball cleanly and throwing it to first. Medalia either wasn't paying attention or didn't care.

"I said move your feet!" He yelled. Clete's eyes opened wide in disbelief, and his arms pinwheeled in confusion. "I did!" he said.

But Medalia had already moved on.

Whoops, Wrong Bottle

If that wasn't enough, the universe decided to pile on. There was a contingent of players on our team who dipped. "Dipping" is baseball slang for using chewing tobacco. I never dipped, but I got familiar with the paraphernalia. The guys had a dip cup, their attempt at a spittoon. They typically used an empty Powerade bottle. One Saturday, the dip cup was sitting on the bench. Clete ran in from the field, mistook the dip cup for his own bottle of Powerade, and started to chug it.

I looked up from my place at second base when the retching started. Clete had lurched from the dugout and was staggering into the bullpen, where he bent at the waist and started vomiting into the grass.

Let the Games Begin

All of our juvenile boundary pushing (or at least some of it) stopped once the games started. We won our first six. I blooped and bounced my way to a decent average. Mike fielded a ball in center field and tried to throw out a runner at home; Clete watched in awe from the pitcher's mound as the ball sailed over the backstop. Brian's eye-black developed more fearsome patterns with each passing day, AJ was a bulldog on the mound, and Frank smiled from the stands.

I remember making a legitimately good play at Everett Memo - rial Stadium. I was playing second base and saw the ball clearly off the bat. It was a high chopper, heavy with topspin. My body took over and moved me to the right, where I slid on one knee, plucked the ball from the dirt and popped to my feet to throw the batter out at first. It was probably the best play I made in my life.

I remember getting heckled at Mountlake Terrace. I was five-foot-seven, one hundred and thirty-five pounds. When I stepped into the batter's box, a group of improbably old-looking guys in the stands behind home plate started chanting, "Rudy! Rudy! Rudy!".

For those of you who don't know, Rudy is the main character in a movie about a small but hard-working young man who goes to great lengths to play for the Notre Dame football team. He is not a college-caliber athlete, but after showing extreme persistence he is eventually allowed onto the team. By the end of his senior season, however, he has never played a down. In his final game, the student section starts chanting "Rudy!" in an attempt to persuade the coach to put him into the game. It works. The stupefied crowd watches as Rudy sacks the opposing quarter-back on the last play of the game, and then they carry him off the field and into the sunset.

At Mountlake Terrace, my cheering section quieted down when I hit a line drive off the fence in left-center.

"That ball would have been out at your place," the shortstop said as I was catching my breath on second base.

"Really?" I said, half in a daze. I hadn't thought it was possible for me to hit a ball that far.

I remember being 6-0 and thinking: "Obviously." This was the team that I had been telling myself I was on for years. In my mind, we weren't performing above our skill set. We were finally showing it.

But then we started to lose. We went to Jackson and got shut down by Travis Snyder, future Toronto Blue Jay. We went to

Shorewood and got shut down by guys who didn't one day make the major leagues. Edmonds-Woodway came to us, and a lot of bad things happened. The year before, future Mariners' prospect Chris Meiniker had hit two home runs against us in the same inning. That had been strangely cool. Senior year, one of their pitchers threw a no-hitter against us. I had the distinction of striking out to end the game. At the time, that wasn't very cool.

Even after losing some games, however, we were still very much in the playoff hunt. My freshman year we had been a 4A school, but by my senior year we had become a 3A school[8], which meant it would be much easier for us to make the postseason. All we had to do was be better than either Lynnwood or Meadowdale —and at the time Lynnwood was not good.

We were well-positioned. As long as we played decent baseball the rest of the way, we would be in the playoffs. If we played well in the early rounds, we might be able to get hot and ride the momentum all of the way to state.

That's when I decided to take a vacation.

I Betray the Team Without Thinking Twice

Aside from baseball, one of my other high school passions was Japanese. I had been taking classes at Shorecrest since I was a freshman. I had also spent ten days on an exchange trip as a sophomore. Senior year, I was offered a chance to go again.

The offer was a ten-day trip to Tokyo, Kyoto, and Osaka with a very small group. It sounded amazing. The only downside was that it would be during spring break—right in the middle of the baseball season. It says something surprising about my priorities that I agreed to go without even thinking.

Before the season started, I wanted to make sure that Coach Medalia knew my plans. I remember sitting on a brown metal chair in his office, my feet planted on the Astroturf rug.

"I just wanted to tell you," I said calmly, "That during spring break I'm going to go to Japan."

I don't remember what he said. I don't think he protested. His eyes may have narrowed as he tried to see whether or not I was serious. It didn't really matter, because my mind was already made up.

When I got back from the trip, I realized that I had missed out on some things. First of all, I had missed out on the day that Clete hit two home runs—one from the right side and one from the left side of the plate.[9] I then missed the pie in the face that Boranger hit him with while he was being interviewed for the local paper.

It turns out I had also missed out on my spot in the lineup. For a period of time, I was on the bench and a talented freshman played second base. At first, I told myself that it made sense.

I'm rusty after ten days off the field. As soon as I get back into form, I'll be back in the lineup.

But then I continued to sit. It dawned on me that perhaps this was punishment for skipping town in the middle of the season. At the time that realization made me a little indignant, but hind - sight makes it look pretty obvious.

The Calm Before the Storm

We didn't finish the season quite as well as we'd started it, but we did do well enough to get into the playoffs. By that time, I had worked my way back into Medalia's good graces and onto the field. Making the playoffs felt like a momentous occasion, and so a good time for reflection. On one of the last practices of the year, we were circled up. Medalia looked at us in his serious way.

"Why do you play baseball?" he asked the team.

Nobody spoke. He turned to me. "Why do you play baseball, Chad?"

I answered without thinking. "Because I like to feel that I'm good at something."

He smiled an unreadable smile. "Do you think you're good at baseball?"

"Yes." I said.

He nodded.

If he had asked me that question one year later, I would have given a very different answer, but at the time I felt it was true.

The Tournament Begins

The district tournament was an hour and a half away in Anacortes, Washington. We trundled into town on our yellow bus and won the first game against a team with purple jerseys. Shaking hands after the game, we knew that one more win would get us into the state tournament.

I could barely contain myself. Was this really happening? The state tournament was the biggest stage I could have imagined playing upon. Reaching it had been my implicit goal for four years, and now it was one game away. I bounced around the house as if lit from within. All we had to do was beat Sedro-Wooley in the next round.

They took the field in blue and white jerseys. It was close until the end.

We lost.

On the ride home, I was angry. Eighteen-year-old boy-men experience a different kind of anger than the rest of us. It's big, incandescent, and powerful—and it wants out. I did what I presume most eighteen-year-olds do when they are angry: wrote a poem. My pen flashed across the page, scorching the paper with illegible black lightning. My hand balled up, and I wanted to smash it into something.

Then a memory leapt into my mind. I saw myself earlier in the year, running down the first-base line in an attempt to beat out a dinky grounder to short. I hit the bag and fell in my theatrical way, landing face-first on the ground. Frustration welled up inside of me, and I slammed my hand into the soft grass.

It hurt surprisingly badly, but the shame was worse than the pain. On the way back to the dugout, I remember feeling deeply embarrassed.

Sitting in the middle of the mostly silent bus, dots connected themselves in my mind. Yes, we had just lost a game. Yes, we might have missed out on our chance to go to State. Yes, I wanted to punch something. But what would that do?

This anger is useless, I thought, and felt that it was true. I closed my notebook, opened my fist, and let the anger drain from me like water from a leaky barrel.

The Tournament Ends

We had a chance to sneak into the state tournament through the losers' bracket, but in the next game, we got demolished by Meadowdale. Clete—playing first base—got hit in the back of the head with an errant throw. He didn't die, but our season did.

On the bus back, this time I felt no anger. People around me sniffled, many of them realizing that they had just played their last baseball game. That wasn't true for me, however. I had been accepted to a small school in eastern Washington called Whit - man College. Its academic reputation drew me in, but because it was such a small school, I also thought I would be able to play baseball there. This was not a small part of its appeal. I hadn't spoken with the coach but had already decided to walk on to the team.

And who knew? Maybe my senior year we'd make the super regionals.

Taking Stock

At that point, I had been playing baseball for thirteen years. I thought of myself as a good player—and not without reason. I wanted to believe that the transition to college ball would be similar to all of the other transitions I had made—rocky at first, perhaps, but with steady improvement over time.

And yet, there was reason to doubt. I knew what it was like to be out of my league. When I imagined the seasons to come, memories of the Woodinville select team floated through my mind. I shook my head in an attempt to shake them out.

Most of those guys were Division I players, I told myself, *but Whitman is a Division III school.*

I'll be fine.

III.

—

WHERE DREAMS GO TO DIE

The Land of the Nerds

WHITMAN COLLEGE IS NOT A PLACE people typically go for the sports. Tucked into the southeastern corner of Washington state in the town of Walla Walla, Whitman is a small school populated by sharp, lovable, and occasionally strange people who tend to value their brains over their brawn.

As such, athleticism was not much of a claim to fame. Whitman doesn't have a football team. When I was there, letterman's jackets didn't exist, and the most anticipated sporting event of the year was the Soccer Party, which involved a lot of beer and no soccer.

And that was fine with me. I wouldn't have been good enough to play baseball at a school with a larger athletics budget. Had I gone to the University of Washington, for example, I wouldn't even have tried out for the team. At Whitman, I sensed that I had a chance to play, and I was excited by it.

At the end of August, my parents buckled me into the backseat of their Saturn VUE, schlepped me across the state, and deposited me and my stuff in the parking lot of a large brick building called Anderson Hall. It was time to grow up[10]. I was not ready. Luckily, I had baseball to keep me sane—or so I hoped.

As soon as the madness of opening week had settled down, I found myself back on the field, grateful for the opportunity to steady my nerves with some ground balls.

Field of Dreams

The field I played on in high school, as you may remember, was bad. It had a mostly grass infield. I could never be sure when a ground ball was going to hit a lump and bounce into my face. The backstop was so tiny that foul balls were constantly flying into the woods. After a few years of pulling weeds and shoveling dirt, I was excited to graduate to college-level facilities.

Sadly, I was in for a few disappointments.

The first came in the fall. Our home stadium was called Borleske, but we couldn't use it for fall practice because it was in use as a high school football field. Instead, we spent the month of September at the dusty diamond of neighboring DeSales High School. Practicing at DeSales felt like going back to Little League. The dugouts were fenced with chain-link, clovers outnumbered blades of grass in the outfield, and the fences were barely three-hundred feet away.

I took solace in the fact that it was only fall ball. Borleske was visible through a small stand of trees, and the sight of the large concrete bleachers down the first-base line was enough to trick me into thinking that it was a real field.

In the meantime, after an upperclassman decided not to return to the team, I found myself in the strange position of being the only player at second base. A younger version of myself might have seen the opportunity and seized it. The eighteen-year-old first year at college version of me, however, was too messed-up.

My entire world was spinning, and even stepping onto the friendly confines of a baseball field didn't make it hold still.

Ground balls bounced off my glove, off my shins, occasionally off my chest, and frequently went right through my legs. My batting eye went cloudy. I didn't hit any balls off any fences. I mostly rolled them to shortstop.

What had happened? Was the game that much faster? Was the competition that much better? It was faster, and it was better, but it's hard to believe that that was the full explanation.

Now I See Me, Now I Don't

Life lessons come in all shapes, sizes, and degrees of desir - ability. The transition from high school to college taught me a somewhat brutal one—no matter who you think you are, some day you probably won't be anymore.

Part of the difficulty with my transition to college was that high school had finished so well. My baseball team won a playoff game. I won the Scholar Athlete of the Year award, gave a well-received speech at an academic awards event, got accepted to the school of my choice, and even had a pretty swell prom date. On some level, I must have thought that I had made it, and that it would be all uphill from there.

On a deeper level, I think I knew that it would not be. Even as high school graduation was approaching, I had the intuition that the world I depended on was about to fall apart. I remember working on final projects and crying inexplicable tears of grief for the mostly functioning life that I was about to lose. What would come next? I had no idea but was worried that it wouldn't be good.

The summer after high school did little to soothe that anxiety. I flunked out of my job as a janitor (effectively) after a few weeks and spent the rest of the summer alone in my backyard, reading fantasy novels and trying not to think about the fall.

When the fall finally came, I found myself scuttling through the brick-lined halls of Whitman College, lonely and afraid. I didn't have many friends yet. I was struggling more in class than I ever had. A horrific crop of acne bloomed on my face. I didn't know who I was, and every ground ball I flubbed made me more confused.

And yet, even though I wasn't playing very well, quitting the team was not an option. Towards the end of fall ball, one of the older guys asked me how things were going. I shrugged. "The baseball team is the closest thing I have to a family here," I said. He nodded in understanding.

Clocking In

After a month, fall practice came to an end, but the training did not stop. It moved from the clover-filled pastures of DeSales High School to the basement of the Sherwood Athletic Center.

At the time, the Sherwood Center was the Whitman gym. Many of the campus buildings were laid in academic brick, but the Sherwood Center was a concrete fortress. A swipe of a student ID card opened the door to the citadel, and down a flight of stairs, past the weight room, and across from the squash courts was the small gym, the place where we tried to learn how to hit.

A few times a week, we would go down there after class, unbundle two long black nets from the wall and unfold them into batting cages. We hit a lot of balls, and as the first semester came to a close, I felt that I had done as much as I could to get ready for the season. I had put on some muscle and was making decent contact in the cage.

But would it translate?

Spring Training

"Spring" practice started in January. We practiced twice a day. The first practice started at six in the morning, just as it had my senior year of high school. Writing this as a mostly domesticated thirty-two-year-old, I wake up relatively easily at around six, but as a mostly feral first-year college student, I definitely did not.

It's hard to put into words exactly how much the eighteen-year-old me hated those six o'clock practices. The sound of my alarm cut into my dreams like a rusty knife, and I woke up angry. Puffs of warm air from the radiator mounted on the wall barely blunted the edge of the Walla Walla morning. I put on gym shorts and my blue and gold Whitman baseball t-shirt and shouldered my gear bag. The cold canvas straps dug into my skin as I trudged through the shadowy hallways of the slumbering dorm—occasionally passing a room that was still awake, partying—and stepped into the frigid darkness of pre-dawn.

And that was just waking-up. Things didn't get better once I got to practice. A strange thing had happened: I had become unable to throw. We practiced in the gym and started by warming up our arms. For some reason, the inside of the gym spooked me, and I couldn't throw the ball to my partner, even from very close range. I repeatedly spiked the ball into the hardwood floor, making him either snag it on the bounce or watch helplessly as it went by. This was very embarrassing. I bore down, trying harder and harder to throw the ball to the middle of my partner's chest. This had the predictable effect of making things worse.

I could take solace in the fact that this is not uncommon in baseball. It's called "getting the yips". Chuck Knoblauch (pronounced Nob-lock), once a Gold Glove second baseman with the Minnesota Twins, got the yips with the Yankees and was never able to recover. John Rocker, closer for the Atlanta Braves, famously couldn't throw the ball to first base, and Rick Ankiel, one-time star pitching prospect for the St. Louis Cardinals, mysteriously lost his ability to throw the ball anywhere near home plate.

The stakes were clearly much higher for those guys, but in a small way I can sympathize with the panic they must have felt watching helplessly as their livelihoods began to slip through their fingers.

Borleske the Beautiful

In the afternoon, we again shouldered our blue bags and made the short trip to Borleske. Finally! I was excited to play on a real college field.

Within a few hours of playing there, however, reality set in. You may remember that the reason we couldn't use Borleske in the fall was that Walla Walla High School had been playing football games there. By January, the goal posts had been removed, but one pesky trace of the football field remained: the yard-markers. Unfortunately, there was no way to get rid of them because they had been dug into the grass, leaving a grid of ruts in the outfield.

The infield was also far from pristine. Like all professional infields, it was a grass diamond surrounded by a fan of dirt (called a "cut-out"). But that didn't mean it was nice. The lips—the places where the grass changes to dirt—were treacherous. If a ball hit one there was no telling where it would go. The dirt itself was hard and mountainous, and at second base ground balls came at me like boulders moving downhill. The area around third base was so uneven that most third basemen moved up to the grass. If they let a ball get to the dirt, it was as likely to wind up in their face as their glove.

It was almost dark by the time we got there, so we ran drills under the lights. It was so cold I could see my breath, and every ball slammed into the palm of my glove like a rock.

On the Road

As January gave way to February, we approached the first games on our schedule. My personal struggles had not resolved themselves, but we had yet to play a game so I didn't know how the team itself would fare.

I knew that there would be some changes. In high school we played games during the week, but in college, we played them on the weekends. Every weekend we had three games, two on Saturday, and one on Sunday. Each game was nine innings. High school games were seven innings, so the transition to the full, professional nine was—at first—exciting.

The length and timing of the games wasn't the only thing that was different. We also traveled much farther to play them. We played half of our games at Borleske, which meant that the other half were on the road. Because Whitman was roughly five hours away from most of the other schools in the conference, road trips became serious. We piled onto the bus on Friday afternoons to head west, dressed in our team-issue polos and whatever excuses for dress pants we owned.

The length of the bus trip paid for itself with a perk: hotels. I remember staying in the same hotel most of the time: Courtyard by Marriott. They had fluffy beds. They had a full breakfast. They had a whiteboard out front that said, "Welcome Whitman Base - ball."

Unfortunately, the teams we played weren't so accommodat - ing. We lost our first game 2-1, which is a very respectable score. We lost our second game 12-0, which is not. As the season unfolded, we had more lopsided results than close ones, and we were usually on the losing end.

I only started five of the thirty-four games and managed a .160 batting average in twenty-five at-bats. I made half as many errors —three—as put-outs at second-base, and spent much of the season shivering and starving on the bench (more about that later). We finished the season 8-26.

It was not a good season, but it was only my first one. As you might expect, I held out hope for the future. My friend Luke and I got together before our sophomore season to talk.

"What do you think we need to do to get better?" I asked him.

He thought about it for a moment and then listed a number of reasonable-sounding, baseball-related things: hit better, field better, pitch better, for example.

"But more than anything else," I remember him saying, "we need to work on our attitude. If we show up to the field expecting to lose, we're going to lose. We've got to change the culture somehow."

I nodded in agreement. By the end of the previous season, I *had* been showing up expecting to lose. Maybe if we believed in ourselves more, we would play better.

The new season started in the middle of February. We lost our first game to Wayland Baptist 10-2. We lost our second game to LaVerne 12-1. We lost our third game to Cal State Eastbay 25-6. It became increasingly difficult to convince myself that mindset was our biggest problem.

Things didn't get any better after the temperature warmed up. We finished the season 3-35.

I did play a little bit better than I had during my first year, but still only managed to hit .195 in eighty-two at-bats. I ended the season with more strikeouts than hits and absolutely no hope for the future.

Early the following year, I had to make a decision. It was my junior year, and a significant percentage of Whitman students studied abroad during that year. I had made up my mind to go to Japan. The question was, For how long? There were two programs: a one-semester program at a school near Osaka and a yearlong program at a school in Kyoto. The yearlong program came more highly recommended, but if I chose that one (assuming I got accepted), I would have to quit baseball.

For some reason, quitting baseball didn't seem like an option. I went to Japan for one semester and packed my glove in my suit - case.

It's worth stopping to think about that. I was one of the worst players on a team that had compiled a record of 11-61 over the two years I had been a part of it. Under the strain of years of poor throwing mechanics, the ligaments in my right shoulder screamed every time I threw a ball. I took little joy in the games and had no illusions that I would ever again be a productive player.

But it didn't matter. Productive or not, I was a baseball player and Whitman was my team. That was enough for me.

When I came back in January, the team had splintered into factions over a leadership dispute. Then, a few weeks into a strained season, I suffered a season-ending injury.

The team went 6-29.

That left one more year. In a strange way, you could say that we saved the best for last.

A Season to Remember

IT STARTED WITH A CALL to the head coach's office.

"Are you sure you want to come back, Chad?" my coach asked. There was legitimate concern in his voice.

I nodded. "Yes."

He leaned back in his chair. "Well," he said after a moment, "if you say so."

I understood his surprise. The previous season had been rough. The atmosphere on the team hadn't been good, and, as usual, we hadn't won very many games. My uncertain status wasn't related to team chemistry or on-field performance, however. It was about coming back from injury. A particularly serious one, in fact. In March, a baseball may have almost killed me.

My Potentially Near Death Experience

It is a day like any other. I put on my baseball pants, stick a Clif Bar in my bag, and go to Borleske. I stretch, half-listening to the other guys bullshit about parties, papers, and Pabst Blue Ribbon, then play catch. The frayed ligaments in my right shoulder sing with every throw. Everything is boring and normal.

Eventually, it is time for batting practice, so we roll out the cage. Somebody takes a screen into shallow center and puts a bucket behind it. I take my place at second base and wait, but there isn't much action. About a half hour in, I field a slow chop - per and lazily turn towards center field to throw it to the bucket guy.

Then my brain detonates. Pain brings me to my knees. My first thought is that I am having a brain aneurysm. I wonder if I'm going to lose the ability to think. Then I wonder if I'm going to lose something even more basic.

But then the flames die down. I find myself on the ground, staring up at the gray eastern Washington sky. People are gath - ered around me. One of them is a trainer.

"Are you OK?" she asks.

I nod, even though I still don't know what has happened. I am so relieved to be alive that I don't really care. She takes me to the dugout and sits me on the bench. It seems very important to answer her questions correctly.

If I get the right answers, that will mean everything is OK.

"Where are you?"

"What day is it?"

"What are you doing here?"

I answer very carefully and get all of them correct. She nods and proclaims me healthy.

I found out later that neither she nor the other trainer on duty saw what had happened. What had happened was that a screaming line drive had hit me in the side of the head.

They sent me home and charged my roommate, Mike, with taking care of me. Mike thought this was a very bad idea. When I refused the Big Cheese pizza he ordered, went into my bed and tried to sleep with my head against the wall, he took me to the hospital.

I spent the next hour inside cocoons of white plastic. Some time later, I was lying propped up in a hospital bed. A nurse walked into the room with a report in her hand.

"You appear to have suffered a skull fracture," she read, "and you show some brain hemorrhaging." My body started to shake uncontrollably at the word "hemorrhaging." Even with my brain partially submerged in its own blood, some part of me knew that it didn't want to hear that.

"If the bleeding doesn't stop, a surgeon will need to remove a part of your skull," she continued. "We can't do that in Walla Walla, so you will be airlifted to a hospital in Seattle."

I was put on a stretcher, loaded into the back of an ambulance, and taken to the airport. From there, I was transferred to the cargo bay of a small airplane. I went in and out of consciousness as the plane flew over the Cascades. In a lucid moment, I heard the two technicians discussing barbecuing techniques. Their disinterest in me was surprisingly reassuring.

The next thing I knew, I was being wheeled through brightly lit corridors. My mom emerged from the halogen glare, probably wild-eyed and stressed out of her mind. Someone in scrubs injected me with what I imagine was a painkiller. I had an immediate allergic reaction to it, and my limbs started contort-ing as if being manipulated by a demented puppeteer. I signaled my intense discomfort with pre-human squeaking noises. Something else was injected into my arm and my body went slack.

I slipped into a series of hospital beds, the smell of antiseptic sanitizing my fever dreams. I awoke at random intervals from the blood-drenched oblivion of my brain and was shuffled to rooms dominated by more large, snowy machines. They filled my mind with white noise, out of which a single thought occasionally emerged: "Am I going to die?"

I had no idea. Luckily, my energy was tied up re-stitching the surface of my brain so there wasn't much left for worry.

After what seemed like forever but was actually one night, I was moved out of the ICU. I sensed that the danger had passed and spent the morning dozing in my room. At one point, I awoke to a middle-aged gentleman sitting in a chair next to my bed. Was he wearing a bowtie? I don't remember, but my instinct is to say yes.

"Hi Chad," he said, smiling. "We're all worried about you."

"Hello," I said, smiling back weakly, recognizing him from photos.

This wasn't a visitor from another world, and it wasn't a hallu-cination. It was only the president.

Of Whitman College, that is—George Bridges. He gave me a copy of *Harper's Magazine* that I was in no condition to read, chatted with me for a few minutes, and then took his leave. I went back to sleep.

I was released from the hospital later that day. Spring break had just begun, but I would not spend this one with my team-mates. I would spend it mostly at home in bed, wondering what was going to happen next.

I slept roughly eighteen hours a day for two weeks. Medical thoughts floated through my foggy mind. *How do they know I'm OK?* I wondered. *Will I know if the bleeding starts again?*

Explicitly religious thoughts followed. *You almost died*, they said. *Now is your chance to repent.* But repent what, exactly? A few things came to mind. I apologized and promised the voices in my head that I would do my best to be good from then on out.

I wondered whether my life would change. Would I emerge from this semi-coma as a different person? If so, would I be a better or a worse one? There was no way to know.

Spring break came to an end, and at least I wasn't dead. I got in the car with my mom and drove back to Walla Walla. When I got to my room, there was a plastic cube on my desk. Inside the cube was a baseball with writing all over it.

3/17/07: Whitman 7 - Willamette 6, it read.

The team won the first game after I got injured and then dedi - cated the victory to me. Everybody signed the ball. It was a pretty nice thing to come back to.

I sat out the rest of the season. My coach released me from practice and away trips, so my afternoons and weekends were more open than they had been since high school. When my teammates came back on Sunday nights, weary from a weekend of getting pummeled, I felt a strange sensation: gratitude for that line drive.

And yet, fast forward to early September and there I was in the coach's office, pledging to come back for more.

No wonder he was surprised. I had even more reason to quit than I'd had the previous year. The fact that I still wanted to play must have struck him as a sign that the brain damage had been permanent.

But my mind was made up. I was a Whitman baseball player. Many of my closest friends were Whitman baseball players. Even though I knew we were going to be bad, I wanted to finish what we had started, no matter how ugly it had become.

Coach nodded and ordered me a special helmet.

Over the years, I had acquired a lot of baseball gear. When I was ten, I got a black and white TPX bat for Christmas. I took it out of the cardboard tube and got so excited that I immediately took a swing at full speed. I'm lucky I didn't kill anybody. I got a silver and blue TPX bat for my seventeenth birthday. I took it out of the cardboard tube and got so excited that I grunted.

When I was eighteen, my glove was stolen out of one of my teammate's cars. His parents were kind enough to give me the money to replace it. I bought a tan Rawlings Pro Preferred, the best glove on the market at the time. When I got to Whitman, I put it in my microwave in a misguided attempt to break it in. The leather got scorched and all of the gel inserts turned to rock. I played with it for as long as I stayed at second base.

All of that said, the helmet became my most prized possession. It was a navy-blue plastic shell stuffed with padding—the same type worn by catchers before hockey-style masks became popu - lar. John Olerud, a smooth-fielding, sweet-swinging Mariners' first baseman and one of my favorite players, also wore one. When I cradled that helmet in my hands, I felt compensated for the injury. How else would I have ever gotten a John Olerud helmet?

I was too skittish to play second base anymore, so I moved to left field. I probably didn't need the helmet out there, but I'd earned it, so I decided to wear it anyway.

Let me tell you a little bit more about the man who ordered it for me.

WHITMAN FAN FEST

Meet Casey Powell

Casey Powell was one of my last baseball coaches. He wasn't quite like any of the others. All of the others took it upon themselves to try to teach us a little bit about baseball and a little bit about life. I'm sure Casey would have liked to do both, but the circumstances didn't make it easy.

Casey knew baseball. He was a former MVP of the conference we played in, and he managed a successful summer league team. He cared about us as players and as people, and I think he did his best to make Whitman a good team. Ultimately, however, he was plagued by too many mismatches.

On the one hand, there were institutional mismatches. Other schools in the conference found a way to help athletes defray the cost of tuition. Whitman apparently did not do that very well.

There were also personality mismatches. He was a straight shooter. We were a group of mostly eccentric weirdos. My friend group told jokes about arcane academic topics or *Snakes on a Plane*. One year, a unique player regaled a recruit with stories of the ghost badger he claimed haunted the gym. Another time, a different guy bet that he could spend a whole day talking like Gandalf. I don't think Casey could really relate.

Unfortunately, the most significant mismatch Casey faced was a mismatch in talent. I played with some very good baseball players at Whitman. Too many of us, however, were over-matched.

We played in the Northwest Conference, a group of Division III schools located mostly around Seattle and Portland. It was a mixed bag of smallish schools, from liberal arts colleges like Lewis and Clark and Linfield to somewhat larger universities like Pacific Lutheran University and the University of Puget Sound. Whitman was the smallest school in the conference, with about 1,500 students at the time I went there (2004–2008). That said, before we started playing games, I'd thought the competition would be relatively equal.

Little did I know that the Northwest Conference is home to some storied D-III baseball programs. Many of the schools were strong, but George Fox and Linfield were perennial power-houses, even on the national stage[11]. Linfield even had a former MLB player for a bench coach. Many of us were over our heads.

That doesn't mean we didn't try, of course. We all tried. Casey tried. As every good baseball coach must, he broke some things (pencils, mostly) during our four years together. We missed bunts, walked the leadoff batter, and struck out looking. When these kinds of things happen, it's conventional wisdom for a coach to "light a fire" under his players. He uses the occasional broken pen or kick to the water bucket to wake them up.

Sadly, you can't wake up a corpse. As soon as Casey stopped getting annoyed (at least visibly), I knew we were dead.

Through it all, he remained a steady presence. I'm sure he was frustrated, both by our play and the constraints placed upon him by the institution. But, in my memory, he never took it out on us. I have nothing but good memories of him as a coach. He left Whitman shortly after I did, moving with his wife and daughters to pastures with fewer goalposts. I hope it was a better fit[12].

Play Ball

Casey ordered my helmet in September. After a few months of practice in left field it was time to start playing games.

We had more of them than in previous years. That year the conference changed its schedule from three games a weekend to four. We would make use of almost all of them on our way to a truly epic losing streak.

That said, it all started with something very unusual: winning.

PRESEASON—WEEK ONE

A New Hope
Los Angeles, California vs Occidental College

We began every season with a trip to warmer climates. Walla Walla bakes in the summer, but it freezes in the winter. Dreaming of southern skies was what got us through January.

We usually went to Arizona, which meant we drove to Seattle, flew south, and stayed in a hotel for a few days. This was no small undertaking. Compared to other groups of similarly aged male athletes, we must have been relatively mild. Just to be safe, however, we had a curfew. At around ten o'clock, a coach would come by and knock on the door to make sure we hadn't gone to a bar or something. Most of the time, everyone was in bed reading a textbook or watching SportsCenter.

My first year, however, there was a problem. We were in Arizona for the pre-season tournament. After a day of games, my roommates and I settled in for the night. We were all present when the coach came for bed check. It turns out that some players weren't, however.

It wasn't exactly that the missing players had gone to a strip club. The coach found them huddled in front of the TV in one hotel room. Maybe they just weren't clear on the rules—maybe they thought they had to be in *someone's* room by ten. That was not the rule, however. When we got back to Walla Walla, we had to run a sprint for every minute they were late (I think it was in the thirties).

I wonder if the punishment would have been as severe if they hadn't been watching porn[13].

My senior year we went to Los Angeles instead of Arizona. I remember waiting outside for our baggage in Burbank, the sun melting the blue sheen of Pacific Northwest winter from my pale face. It was so pleasant I felt like I was dreaming. I turned to Laz, our sophomore catcher and southern California native. I don't know if I had ever spoken to Laz before, or had even heard him utter a complete sentence. He was beaming beneath his dark sunglasses.

"Feels good to be home, eh?" I said.

His smile got even wider. "Yeah," he said.

A day later our bus arrived at Occidental College. As we strolled beneath the palm fronds towards the baseball field, we heaved a collective sigh of regret. Marveling at the amount of skin on display in the second week of February, I assume I wasn't the only one wishing he had applied there.

What happened next was even more shocking: we won.

Twice!

We played three games that weekend. When the dust settled, the preternaturally warm winter sun shone on a Whitman team with a winning record. It was the first time we had had one in my four years on the team. An old, now unfamiliar feeling awoke inside of me: hope.

We tried to act natural. We told ourselves that we had just taken two out of three from a good team, which meant that we must have been an even better team. Occidental finished the season with 15 wins, so they must have been at least a decent team. We, on the other hand, wouldn't win another game for two and a half months.

The Results

Date	Score
2/09/08	Whitman 3 – 6 Occidental (L)
	Whitman 5 – 4 Occidental (W)
2/10/08	Whitman 11 – 10 Occidental (W)

Record

W	L
2	1

Meet Coach Van Dyke

From finding recruits to administering bed checks, running a college baseball program is hard work. Casey couldn't have done it all by himself. He had a few assistants, but the one I remember most fondly is Coach Van Dyke.

Van Dyke was one of my all-time favorite coaches. I don't think he taught me a lot about baseball[14]. He did, however, make me smile at a time when I desperately needed to.

Before practice after a particularly bad weekend, he asked us to sit down.

"It's a simple game, fellas," he said.

I can't tell you how often baseball coaches start their speeches like that. "It's a simple game, fellas," they say, and then they tell you to do a bunch of really difficult things.

"Here's how it works," Van Dyke said. "First, you get a runner on base."

Ok.

"Then, you bunt him over."

Reasonable.

"Then, you hit him in."

He smiled, spreading his arms wide as if he had just given us a very valuable gift. "And that's it!"

We didn't have anything to say, which was fine because he still had plenty.

"One run an inning," he said. "It's that simple. If you do that, how many runs will you get?"

Was it a rhetorical question, or did he actually want us to do the math?

"Nine runs," he said finally.

I blinked. Nobody else said anything.

"How many games would we win if we scored nine runs?" he continued.

If we were any other team, the answer would have been most of them. Unfortunately, we regularly lost by double digits, so even scoring nine runs a game we would have lost all of the time.

Coach Van Dyke was a buoy of good cheer bobbing in a sea of despair. He regularly got over-excited at the third-base coaching box, waving runners home only to have them thrown out by ten feet. Perhaps overcompensating for these lapses in judgment, on multiple occasions he grabbed a runner going by and pulled him onto the base. This, unfortunately, is against the rules and results in said runner immediately being called out.

Eventually, Casey stopped letting him go over there and moved him to the first-base box instead. "Hard ninety!" he yelled from foul territory, encouraging us to hustle out every dribbler to short and dinker to the pitcher.

One responsibility commonly given to assistant coaches is throwing batting practice. Van Dyke's batting practice arm was legendary. He would get behind an L-screen, pluck a ball from the bag, and then fling it towards home plate. Sometimes it made it into the strike zone, but it was almost as likely to hit the batter. One time, he missed the batting cage entirely; the ball almost made it into the first-base dugout.

I appreciated Van Dyke's approachability, persistence, and genuinely friendly spirit. My time at Whitman wouldn't have been nearly as fun without him.

Chinks in the Armor
McMinnville, Oregon @ the Linfield Invitational

Fresh off of our success in southern California, we rolled into the suburban oasis of McMinnville, Oregon for a preseason tournament feeling uncharacteristically good about ourselves.

They say that you're never as bad as you feel on a losing streak and never as good as you feel on a winning streak. It's possible that we were exactly as bad as we would later feel during our losing streak, but the two-game winning streak definitely went to our heads. In fact, it sat on our shoulders like a large bird of prey. We got off the bus ready to let it loose. Unfortunately, as soon as the hood came off, the falcon started pecking our eyes out.

The Results

Date	Score
2/22/08	Whitman 3 — 7 Linfield (L)
2/23/08	Whitman 3 — 13 Concordia (L)
2/10/08	Whitman 3 - 11 University of Puget Sound (L)

Record

W	L	Losing Streak
2	4	3

Our winning streak was over, and our losing streak had just begun. It was a road-trip, however, so at least we had Kangaroo Court.

Trial by Fine

Kangaroo Court was the highlight of every road-trip and provides a clear illustration of how certain young men bond. It allowed us to show love and affection for each other after first masking it with contempt—while also sometimes just letting us be mean to each other in an officially sanctioned way.

Court was held on Saturday night in one of the upperclass-men's hotel rooms. At the beginning of each session, people would scribble down claims against one of their teammates. After all claims were in, one of the upperclassmen would pick them out of a hat and read them aloud as theatrically as possible. The claimant would elaborate on the story, the defendant would try to say something funny enough to absolve himself, and then the jury would vote. If the verdict was guilty, the judge would assign a fine, generally a couple of quarters, that went towards beer for a party at the end of the season.

What type of claims went into the hat? Well, just as physical humor gets the readiest laughs, the simplest type of claim was for embarrassing physical mistakes. Did someone try to dive for a ground ball and wind up belly-flopping in an embarrassing way? That would have been a fine. One time during my senior year, I drilled a line drive into right-center and got so excited—at this point my batting average was probably under .100—that I tripped and slammed into the ground two steps out of the batter's box. I had to half-stumble, half-crawl to first base. That was definitely a fine. Luckily, I was safe at first, otherwise the fine might have been much worse.

Another class of fine was for breaking unwritten rules. While ridiculous people in a number of ways, we did have standards. Kangaroo Court was a way of policing them. Did someone wear a muscle shirt to practice? That was a fine. Did someone step on the bus with a mustache? Fine. Did someone forget his belt and have to borrow one from a coach? Heavy fine.

In addition to these two, there was a final class of fine which could only be described as the entirely unreasonable, completely arbitrary, and fully inescapable fine. With the other two classes of fines, a well-mounted defense could get a defendant off the hook. This final type, however, was exempt from due process. There was a reason for that: it was the fine levied against the guys who were squeaky clean.

Some people never seem to do anything wrong. They hustle all the time, come to practice fully dressed, get bunts down, don't trip over themselves, and never miss a sign. The thing about the kind of male bonding that happens at Kangaroo Court is that it's not fun unless everybody gets whacked. In the event that a person presented no obvious flaw, it was customary to create one out of thin air.

One otherwise impeccable player was fined for the amount of bacon he consumed at breakfast. Another player was fined for making too much money playing internet poker. Yet another player was fined for having two hundred dollars stolen from him.

That last player was me.

Before every road trip we received meal money, somewhere between fifteen and twenty dollars a day. To an eighteen-year-old who had never held a job for more than a month, that seemed like a serious salary, so in my first year I decided to save it.

Before getting on the Friday afternoon bus, I went to the student store and used my meal plan (which is to say, my parents' money) to purchase a large number of granola bars and protein shakes. I planned to use these items to carry me through the weekend so that I could pocket the meal money.

While perhaps thrifty, this was not a very healthy plan. Protein shakes and granola bars are not enough to fuel a person during normal activities; they certainly aren't enough to play two nine-inning baseball games on. To make matters worse, I couldn't pull myself out of bed in time to eat the free breakfast at the hotel. If kind parents hadn't provided lunch at every game, I might have passed out.

Even with the free lunches, I ended up wasting away. My skin turned to wax, and my energy levels plummeted. If there's one thing I am willing to do, however, it's to suffer for something I believe in. For whatever reason I believed in banking those forty bucks, so I did it.

I didn't spend them, though. I actually didn't even bank them. I simply put them in my wallet and left them there. By the end of the season, I had lost ten pounds but gained over two hundred dollars.

Sadly, I didn't get to use any of it.

One Sunday evening after a long weekend of losing, I went into my bag to fish out my wallet. After a few moments of sifting through moldy t-shirts and crusty blue socks, I started to worry. I dumped the contents of the bag onto the floor of my dorm room. There were balled-up batting gloves, strips of tape, two gloves, empty Gatorade bottles, a pair of shoes I had been searching for and plenty of dirt—but no wallet.

I sent Casey an email to ask if anybody had found it. Maybe I had put it in the wrong bag by mistake. He asked everyone to check. Nobody found it. The wallet never materialized. Some-body somewhere bought a lot of beer with my year's-worth of food money. I hope they had a fun party.

I certainly learned a lesson. For the next three years, I didn't save a penny of the meal money. This meant a lot of Chicken McNuggets and Arby's Roast Beef Sandwiches, but oh well.

After the episode faded from memory, somebody brought it up at Kangaroo Court and I got fined.

The week after our loses at the Linfield Tournament, we trav - elled to Central Washington. It was only a day trip, so we didn't have Kangaroo Court and I don't remember whether or not we got meal money. What we did get was probably more valuable: a really good laugh.

PRESEASON—FINAL SERIES

Bait and Switch
Ellensburg, Washington vs Central Washington University

The Wildcats were taking batting practice when we showed up.

Pump-up music blared from the speakers behind home plate as the large, bearded men who were supposedly our contempo - raries bashed baseballs to Linkin Park, Metallica, and Rage Against the Machine. The PA system at Borleske was so low-quality that it would have blown up if we'd tried to play music through it, so I was excited by the novelty.

We didn't get to hit to Linkin Park, however—the Wildcats had a special soundtrack for us. As soon as we took the field, the prog rock was replaced by the cotton-candy notes of a synthesizer.

"Hiya, Barbie!"

You've got to be kidding me, I thought.

"Life in plastic, it's fantastic!"

We hit to Avril Lavigne, Britney Spears, and the Backstreet Boys. The Central guys must have had a great time watching us, but in a weird way the joke was on them. Their attempt to emas -

culate us failed, if only because we had already been fully emas -
culated by three and a half years of losing a lot.

Ellensburg is roughly two and a half hours away from Walla
Walla, so rather than paying for a bus, when we went to Central
we took vans. Casey drove one, and an assistant coach usually
drove another. Senior year, Coach Van Dyke turned off the high -
way and onto the main drag for the last time. A pitcher named
Sam read aloud—as he liked to do—the names of restaurants as
we passed them.

"McDonald's, Burger King, Wendy's, Jack in the Box..."

Did we think we were going to win? I think we had a hope.
Some of the afterglow from the Occidental series remained,
occasionally warming at least my heart like an old coal.

"Subway, Skippers, Baskin and Robbins..."

We parked, unloaded the vans, and trudged through the ever-
present 30 mph wind to the baseball field. An hour later they
turned off the Mariah Carey and the umpire said play ball. We
almost won one. Then they kicked our butts.

The Results

Date	Score
3/02/08	Whitman 9 – 10 Central Washington (L)
	Whitman 1 – 12 Central Washington (L)

Record

W	L	Losing Streak
2	6	5

Meet Sam Thompson

I've never seen anyone throw a baseball quite like Sam. In college, he was a large human being, standing over six-feet tall and probably weighing close to two hundred pounds. When he stood on the mound and glared at the catcher, I felt fear for the batter. That was in large part because I had no idea where the ball was going to go.

Sam was a mechanical model of a hurricane, no two deliveries ever appearing exactly alike. The ball emerged from the chaos of his limbs and flew towards home plate with equal probability of being a strike, in the dirt, or behind the batter.

Sam was one of the few people who didn't let Whitman baseball get him down. No matter what happened, no matter how many errors his defense made behind him, no matter how many times his catchers told him to stop walking the leadoff batter, Sam was happy. Yes, some people probably would have liked him to care more about his mechanics, but anybody who can take the poundings we took and still somehow be at peace with his life is doing something right.

In fact, Sam was shrouded in many layers of mystery. His past was legendary. He was said to have thrown a no-hitter in high school. He was said to have batted over four hundred. He was also said to have played in a conference where some of the schools were too small to find nine players, and to have thrown the no-hitter against a school for the blind[15].

His present was equally interesting. A rare theater major, I had no idea how he spent his hours off the field. Was he building sets? Was he writing scripts? Was he standing in front of an audience, reciting soliloquies? I didn't and still don't know. What I do know is that he liked to say the names of fast-food restaurants and that he was well-loved by his fellow pitchers.

The role of pitchers changes over time. In Little League, pitchers are generally the best athletes on the team. When they're not pitching, they play shortstop or centerfield. In high school, it is more or less the same. In college and beyond, however, pitchers specialize. Baseball is a hard game. Hitting is hard. Fielding is hard. Pitching is very hard. If you don't spend most of your time practicing your one thing, then you will probably be bad at everything.

In college, the team separates into pitchers and position players. I don't know what pitchers think of position players, but position players think pitchers are weird. It's a trope, as much as anything.

But then again pitchers *are* kind of weird. They only play every once in a while. Most of the time, they sit in the bullpen and screw around, or they sit behind home plate with a radar gun and screw around. From the perspective of a position player, pitchers seem to do three things: run, throw, and screw around.

Perhaps as a result of their isolation, pitchers do something else: bond. My memories of Sam are inextricable from my memories of his relationships with the other pitchers. Whether it was his mentoring of Sease, his adoration of PJ, or his weirdly submissive relationship with Keali'i, Sam was a pitcher among pitchers.

REGULAR SEASON—WEEK ONE

Here We Go Again
Tacoma, Washington vs University of Puget Sound Loggers

After our trip to Central, the regular season began with a trip west. We traveled to Tacoma to play the University of Puget Sound Loggers.

As a Whitman student, I felt compelled—for better or worse—to think about mascots. At the time, Whitman had one of the most incongruous mascots imaginable: a missionary. I suppose at one point it had made sense because the school was founded by one, an influential local figure named Marcus Whitman.

That said, it isn't exactly a mascot for the 21st century, espe‑cially not at a liberal institution like Whitman. I don't remember seeing the mascot anywhere. There *was* an old t-shirt floating around that featured a young Marcus Whitman (perhaps) holding a Bible in one hand and brandishing a pistol in the other, his young wife, Narcissa, latched onto one arm. This shirt was much sought after, though perhaps not for pious reasons. Aside from the hunt for that shirt, pride in the school mascot manifested itself in only one place: the chant, "Missionaries, Missionaries, we're on top!"

I remember wondering what to make of the Logger as a mascot. Trees are good, right? But then again so are tables and chairs. What I can say for sure is that when Logger met Mission‑ary, the burly lumberjacks beat the men of God around the field with a 2 x 4.

The Results

Date	Score
3/08/08	Whitman 1 — 14 Puget Sound (L)
	Whitman 4 — 8 Puget Sound (L)
3/09/08	Whitman 3 — 10 Puget Sound (L)
	Whitman 2 — 8 Puget Sound (L)

Record

W	L	Losing Streak
2	10	9

Interlude: A Good Thing Happens

The season, which had gotten off to such a promising start, was beginning to take a nose dive. The losses would pile up for another month and a half, but on my birthday—March 12th—two good things happened.

The first came right before practice. Seated around a battered coffee table in my friends' room, I won my first ever game of Settlers of Catan. I looked down at the long orange blocks that marked my road. I looked at my cities, counted, and then re-counted my Victory Points.

10.

I really have 10, right?

I did.

It was the first time I had won at anything in what seemed like a lifetime. I raised my arms to the sky, basking in the unfamiliar glow of victory, and then went upstairs to change into my prac - tice gear.

That is where the second good thing happened.

I had been playing baseball for seventeen years at that point and had experienced many things on the diamond. I had dislo - cated my shoulder, been hit in the face with a bat, been drilled in the chest with a ball while sliding into home plate, and, of course, been hit in the side of the head with a line drive. I had a few game-winning hits under my belt, nestled right next to a few game-losing errors and strikeouts. The one thing I had never done, however, was hit a ball over a fence.

I'd come close a few times. In Little League, as you might remember, I had one easy in-the-park homer—until I was called out for (supposedly) missing third base. In high school, I hit the fence at Mountlake Terrace and put a few balls off the warning track at Shorecrest. Sadly, in college I rarely hit the ball out of the infield.

However, on this day that would change. During batting prac-tice, I took an unusually mighty swing. I made solid contact and then—watched as the ball sailed over the left-field fence. It's usually bad form to watch your batting practice shots too intently. I was so locked on to that ball, however, that I didn't even swing at the next pitch. I don't think Casey minded very much.

Someone retrieved the ball for me, and I signed it.

From: Chad

To: Chad

Happy 22nd Birthday.

It was a triumphal day in the midst of persistent failure. Unfortunately, all of the gains would be wiped out by a disas-trously ill-conceived encounter with a gravity bong later that evening. That was probably fitting.

REGULAR SEASON—WEEK TWO

Go Away, Scott Brosius
Walla Walla, Washington vs The Linfield College Wildcats

Linfield College was a team we probably shouldn't have had to play.

At the time, they had won National Championships in 1966 and 1971, and they have since won another (2013). Former New York Yankee and World Series MVP, Scott Brosius, was one of their assistant coaches. Once, someone scorched a ground ball into the Linfield dugout. Brosius casually reached out and snagged it with a bare hand. I could hardly believe such a thing was humanly possible.

It wasn't just the presence of a major leaguer on their coaching staff that made Linfield formidable, however. Their players were also good. I didn't learn any of their names because they felt less like peers than beings from a higher plane of existence. It was just one nameless Wildcat after the next, pounding balls to the fence, running around the bases, and touching home plate.

We didn't beat Linfield once in my four years at Whitman. They were Casey's alma mater, so I know he would have liked to get one win against them. Senior year, at least we got close.

The Results

Date	Score
3/15/08	Whitman 2 – 3 Linfield (L)
	Whitman 0 – 5 Linfield (L)
3/16/08	Whitman 0 – 10 Linfield (L)
	Whitman 4 – 13 Linfield (L)

Record

W	L	Losing Streak
2	14	13

WHITMAN FAN FEST

Meet Luke Marshall

Luke had one of his most painful baseball moments against Linfield College. He was playing left field at their place, and someone mashed a ball in his direction. He turned and ran, thinking he could track it down. The ball went way over the fence. Unfortunately, Luke ran directly into it.

It's hard to say that it was his fault. He was chasing a ball he thought he could catch and wasn't looking for the fence. In situations like these, outfielders are supposed to take care of each other. If one outfielder sees another approaching a fence, it's his job to let his teammate know. Luke was playing left. Did the centerfielder tell him he was getting close to the fence?

No. The ball had been crushed. Why make a fuss, the center-fielder presumed, when it was obvious that nobody could catch it?

Luke was one of the best all-around players we had, especially his junior year. He hit for average[16], had good gap power, and possessed both a solid throwing arm and good instincts in the outfield.

The one tool he didn't have was speed. Luke chugged around the outfield like a tugboat. You could be sure he was going to get to the spot, but you couldn't guarantee that the ball would still be in the air by the time he did.

Luke double-majored in physics and philosophy, so it's perhaps no surprise that he was the most psychologically mature of all of us. He exuded a very comforting "dad" aura. I remember one night sitting on a couch in his room. It was senior year. He was reading Kierkegaard or something. I was whining about growing up.

"Can you believe we'll have to get jobs soon?"

He didn't look up from his book.

"We might even have to put on ties," I grimaced in disgust.

"It's just a tie," he said, again without looking up.

"Yeah, I guess," I said, a little bit pouty. But it felt good to be put in my place.

He was jolly in a way that was alien to my weak, English-major cynicism. One summer, we spent two weeks driving down the west coast, visiting Minor League baseball stadiums on our way to a Mariners/A's series in Oakland. We camped once or twice. At one of the campgrounds, Luke befriended a sixty-year-old man named Richie. Richie regaled us with stories of all the gophers he had blasted out of the ground with his revolver. Together, he and Luke drank whiskey, listened to country music, and slapped their knees with laughter that echoed into the night.

Everyone weathers their own storms, and I'm sure that Luke has had his rainy days, but in action he was (and remains) one of the steadiest people I know. No matter how crappy we played or how banged up he was, Luke was always there.

Spring Break

After the Linfield series, it was time for spring break. Spring break was always interesting. We got time off from class, but not from baseball. Because the dorms closed, the underclassmen moved into rooms in one of the frat houses. Put a large number of guys in a run-down house for two weeks with nothing to do but play baseball poorly and strange things will happen.

Sophomore year, four of us decided that it would be a good idea to dye our hair. We went to Bartell Drugs and combed through the boxes of Revlon, discarding Ash Blonde (too much bleach), Chestnut Brown (too natural), and Carrot Red (too bold) before ultimately settling on Raven Black.

We bought it and went into the main bathroom with our shirts off. It took us a while to figure out how to put on the hair nets and get the gloopy black chemicals into the bottle. A few people walked in and then promptly walked back out. We managed to get the goo onto and washed from our heads. I looked into the mirror. My normally dirt-colored hair was now a gleaming shade of black.

The next day at practice, we decided to play a joke on our coach. We stood next to each other during the pre-practice meeting and slowly removed our hats. At first Casey didn't notice. We scratched our heads, doing everything we could to draw his attention to our now raven-colored locks. Eventually he noticed. His eyes narrowed, and then a pained look appeared on his face.

"Did you bozos dye your hair?" He said.

We began to giggle uncontrollably. He shook his head as if small, mischievous children were running around on the surface of his brain, punching holes in it with their rubber cleats. "Put your hats on," he said with a sigh and went back to detailing the mostly hopeless practice plan.

Two of my co-conspirators that year were Adam and Kramer. At the time they were sharing a room in Douglas Hall. They were simultaneously a match made in heaven and in hell. They loved each other. They hated each other. They watched The Office and smoked cheap cigars together, and then they called each other cruel names while playing Mario Kart 64 together. I often slept between their beds on a couch we repeatedly stole from a lounge area, occasionally ducking beneath a blanket to avoid flying objects. Here's a little bit more about each of them.

WHITMAN FAN FEST

Meet Adam Knappe

Adam was one of our infielders. He is a great athlete, but you might not notice right away because he is such a stellar mathlete. When he wasn't taking grounders at Borleske, he was in his room memorizing the shapes of molecules and the breeding patterns of lizards.

Adam loved baseball deeply, but his greatest love was reserved for the natural world. One summer at Whitman, we were hiking in Western Oregon. We lugged backpacks stuffed with peanut butter and jelly sandwiches up heavily forested inclines, appreciating all of the green things on display around us. The most enchanting green things were fluffy patches of moss carpeting the sides of the trail. They looked so soft and springy that I felt a powerful urge to romp through them.

Will I bounce? I wondered. I bent my knees, poised to leap in, but Adam had read my mind and was not happy about what he'd seen.

"Don't touch the moss!" he said.

The ferocity in his voice made me stiffen. My knees locked up just before lift-off. *Abort!* I thought, and backed away, feeling like a third-grader who had been caught about to climb a church organ.

"What's the big deal?" I said sullenly. "It's just moss."

That was not the right thing to say.

"Just moss?" he said, indignation flying from him in sparks. "I'll have you know that...." and then he started lecturing me about biodiversity and other things I now appreciate but didn't at the time. Suffice it to say that I didn't get to play in the moss.

That wasn't the only time I experienced his fierce love for little living things. His family had a condo in Ocean Shores, a rickety community on the rocky coast of Western Washington. One starry night, we were driving back to the condo from town. All of a sudden Adam swerved violently on the narrow road, sending his battered, white Mazda Protegé into the other lane.

I tensed, fear squeezing my muscles into knots. He swerved back onto our side of the road, stopped the car, and got out. He ran back the way we'd come, not even bothering to shut the door.

What is going on? I wondered, turning around to watch him. He jogged to a spot a few yards back, bent down in the middle of the road, and then turned back to the car. What had we run over? Adam had a grin on his face by the time he made it back. He showed us the tiny green frog that was sitting in the palm of his hand.

"Look at this, guys!" he said, beaming. "I can't believe I almost ran him over!"

Upon meeting this young, bearded naturalist—with his goofy smile, love of the symphony, and subscription to *Harper's*—you would be forgiven for not realizing that he could hit. But he could. He wasn't six-foot-five, so I imagine that few pitchers felt fear when he stepped into the batter's box. But then he hit plenty of line drives right past them into center field. By the end of his time at Whitman, he had actually matured into a very solid player. We could have used a few more like him.

WHITMAN FAN FEST DOUBLE HEADER

Meet Kramer Phillips

Where Adam had a love for tree frogs and Stephen Jay Gould, Kramer had a love for Dave Matthews Band and JFK.

Believe it or not, the person who first introduced me to Kramer was Frank. It was the summer before our first year at Whitman. I was sitting on Frank's deck, eating a hamburger. Frank looked up when the sliding glass door to the kitchen banged open behind me. A smile touched his face, as if he knew I was in for a treat.

"Frisky," he said, rising from his seat, "I'd like you to meet somebody."

He pointed and I turned to see a tall, gangly kid coming out from the kitchen.

"This is Kramer Phillips," he said. "He'll be joining you at Whitman."

Kramer ended up living just down the hall from me during our first year. Perhaps thanks to the blessing from Frank, he quickly became one of my closest friends.

Kramer rubbed off on me in a number of ways, but the clearest impact he had was upon my iTunes library. At the time, he was the most unabashed Dave Matthews Band fan on earth. Up until that point I'd had no opinion of Dave Matthews Band, but after meeting Kramer it wasn't long until I was illegally scouring the college network for every scrap of Dave I could find.

Kramer didn't rub off on me in a number of other ways. His fashion sense was solidly New England chic. I was only comfortable in jeans and a t-shirt. He was involved in politics. I don't think I knew who the president was.

Perhaps the biggest difference between the two of us, however, was that he was really good at baseball. The second he stepped onto the field as a first-year, he became one of the top five players on the team. Like Adam, he didn't look like a jock. He was tall but weighed about 120 pounds. His movements were efficient but not graceful. He still had braces.

But he was good. He didn't make errors at second base, and he smacked fastballs to the fence, making his crane-like way into second for plenty of doubles.

Perhaps you remember Coach Van Dyke. Van Dyke loved everybody in his own way, but he loved Kramer the most. I think it had as much to do with his name as his gap power.

"Kramer!" he said on the first day of practice freshman year.

"Hey, coach," Kramer said.

"Your name is Kramer!" Van Dyke said again. You could almost see the scenes from Seinfeld playing in his mind's eye.

"Sure is," Kramer said.

Van Dyke chuckled. "I'm going to call you Cosmo."

"Whatever you want," Kramer said.

I don't think he ever said the name "Kramer" again.

"HEY COSMO!"

Van Dyke said it so often and with so much enthusiasm that we couldn't help but imitate him.

"Nice hit, COSMO!"

"Great play, COSMO!"

"Go to hell, COSMO!" (That was Adam).

I'm surprised that Van Dyke—not to mention Casey—didn't die when Kramer told him he was done after sophomore year.

But who can blame him, really? That year we lost our first twenty-four games.

> The team wasn't the same after Kramer left. We were worse
> statistically, without a doubt, but also a fair amount less fun. I'm
> happy to have had him as a teammate for even two years.

Sophomore year we dyed our hair during spring break, but senior year the first week of break passed without incident. On Friday, we traveled to Portland for a weekend series against Pacific University.

REGULAR SEASON—WEEK THREE

It All Starts to Blur Together
Forest Grove, Oregon vs The Pacific University Boxers

One time, a guy from Pacific hit a home run against us that didn't go over the fence. It wasn't an inside-the-park home run, either. Our right fielder caught it.

There was a large tree in right field whose branches hung over the fence. "If a ball hits any part of the tree," the umpires told Casey during their pregame meeting, "it's a home run."

Well, whatever, he must have thought. *That's not going to happen.*

And then, late in a rare, relatively close game, one of the Boxers hit a high fly ball to right field. Our right fielder—a tall, lanky guy named Shultz—backed up to the fence. He reached up, snagged the ball, and slammed into the wall.

"Home run!" the umpire said.

Shultz held up his glove, the universal signal for "I caught it." The ball was definitely inside. The umpire shrugged and pointed to the tree. The leaves were rustling. Casey came out to argue. Shultz was beside himself. Everyone on the bench was scratching something. But the umpires didn't budge.

"Rules are rules," they said, and I guess they were right.

The Results

Date	Score
3/21/08	Whitman 3 - 9 Pacific (L)
	Whitman 0 - 23 Pacific (L)
3/22/08	Whitman 6 - 7 Pacific (L)
	Whitman 3 - 5 Pacific (L)

Record

W	L	Losing Streak
2	18	17

After the series with Pacific, we came back from Portland. Even though it was still spring break, I looked forward to sleeping in my own bed because at that point I was already living in a frat house.

After junior year, catcher/pitcher Mike Rathwell and I had moved from our off-campus house into a room on the second floor of the TKE house. TKE stands for Tau Kappa Epsilon, which are the letters of the fraternity I had somewhat inexplicably joined my freshman year.

All of the rooms in that house have names. There was The Bat Cave, The Romper Room, The President's Room, The Blue Room, The Attic, and a whole lot of other rooms whose names I don't remember. Mike and I moved into The Fireplace Room, so named because of a large, defunct fireplace in one corner.

On the mantle, there were two or three rows of empty Jäger - meister bottles. It was customary for the occupants of The Fire - place Room to undertake something called the Jäger Challenge, which was basically two people drinking a bottle of Jägermeister as fast as they could. I think the record was under two minutes, which may be as fast as you can possibly pour out a bottle of Jägermeister. Mike and I declined the challenge.

We had to stay sober so that we could play our best baseball, of course.

Meet Mike Rathwell

Our first year, Mike and I lived in different dorms and so didn't immediately become close friends. I remember meeting him for the first time on the steps of the TKE house. He looked serious. He made jokes. I was intimidated.

Before coming together on the baseball diamond, we crossed paths on a different playing field. In the fall, Ankeny Field, the large patch of grass in the center of campus, was transformed into the site of the most intense athletic competition anyone experienced at Whitman—intramural flag football. I played on the E-Section team, and Mike quarterbacked the team from 2-West. I remember him as the kind of annoying guy who threw passes and really wanted to win.

Baseball players were forbidden from playing flag football after our sophomore year, in small part, perhaps, because I managed to completely and dramatically dislocate my left shoulder reaching for somebody's flag in a game against Mike's team. That was the last time that we were ever on opposite sides of the ball.

You could say that Mike and I bled into each other. At least, he bled into me. We were both ambivalent English majors. We took a class on Irish poetry together and bonded over bogs and W. B. Yeats. I later took a Shakespeare class without him, but by that point we were already linked. During a project, one of my group members squinted at me and asked, "Do you know Mike Rathwell?"

"Actually, I live with him," I said, a little taken aback.

She snapped her fingers. "I knew it! You two are like the same person."

We aren't the same person—he is deeply rational whereas I tend to just follow my nose—but we were both undersized baseball players whose best teams seemed to be behind them.

Mike has one of the most incisive minds of anyone I've ever met—and zero tolerance for bullshit. Because the Whitman baseball team was at least 90% bullshit, I imagine he was in pain most of the time. Luckily, he also has one of the sharpest senses of humor of anyone I've ever met, which saved him and us.

Humor was what kept us alive. In the middle of April, when we'd lost dozens of games, our team batting average was sinking to zero and our team ERA ballooning to infinity, if we couldn't laugh then we would have been forced to cry (or punch each other). There wasn't much to laugh at other than ourselves, so we became very good at self-deprecating humor.

Mike's was the best. He was a catcher, and one of his favorite themes to riff on was the irreparable damage the Whitman pitching staff was doing to his fertility. The more balls they threw in the dirt, the more balls he took to the nuts. With every trip behind the plate, he half joked, his chances of one day becoming a father went down[17].

Just like Kramer, Mike got a special nickname from Van Dyke. Following the hallowed tradition of baseball nicknames, they were never very creative. Kramer's (Cosmo) was by far the most original. Adam became "Knappey." Luke became "Lukey." Sam became "Sammy." I became "Frisky."

Mike (Rathwell) had the bad luck of becoming "Ratty".

Without Mike, I don't know that I would have made it all the way through Whitman baseball; without Whitman baseball, I don't know that I would have become such good friends with Mike. Sometimes things work out in strange ways.

Currently he is one of the guiding forces behind Driveline Baseball, a company that uses data and heavy baseballs to help
pitchers throw harder while hurting their shoulders less.

The Gray Havens

Mike and I didn't have to move out of our room during spring
break, which was convenient. It's possible that we could have
used the change of scenery, however.

One day I got bored. We were sprawled across battered leather
couches in The Six Pack, watching March Madness.

"Gentlemen!" I said suddenly. I'd had an idea.

They grunted.

"I offer you a wager."

I addressed them in my best Gandalf voice. It sounded more
like a bad Sean Connery impersonation. They were confused, but
only a little bit.

"I bet five dollars that I can talk in my Gandalf voice for the rest
of the day."

That's right: I had nothing to do with the ghost badger, but the
Lord of the Rings weirdo was me.

"You're an idiot," they said, without taking their eyes from the
game.

"Then it's settled!"

I thought it would be easy. The Lord of the Rings was almost my
religion. I attended the premiere of *The Return of the King* dressed
as a hobbit. I could recite the majority of *The Fellowship of the Ring*
from memory. How hard could it be to talk like Gandalf for eight
hours?

For the first five minutes, I had a great time. "Fool of a Wildcat!"
I yelled at the TV (Arizona was playing).

"You shall not pass that defense!" I exclaimed.

They flashed a shot of Michael Jordan sitting courtside, wearing his NBA championship rings. "Don't tempt me, Michael!" I said, recoiling from the TV.

The act got old very fast. I quickly ran out of one-liners and crafting original speech in the Gandalf voice was surprisingly difficult. I stopped speaking and sat on the couch in increasingly sullen silence until the game ended and we changed to go to practice.

I was very unhappy, but I wasn't going to lose the bet. I resolved to say nothing for the entire two and a half hours. Unfortunately, it wasn't going to be that easy. We circled up for the daily meeting and somebody—probably Adam—turned to Casey.

"Hey coach," he said. "Ask Chad something."

Oh no, I thought. *Please don't.*

Casey was suspicious. "Why?"

"Just do it," probably-Adam said.

Casey sighed.

"What is it this time?"

"Well," I said, trying to sound enough like Gandalf to keep the bet alive but not so much like Gandalf that I would have to run laps, "I have to talk like—"

He cut me off. "I don't care."

As the circle broke up and we were walking to play catch, one of my friends, probably Luke, approached me.

"Hey," probably-Luke said.

"Yes?" I said, weary.

"I'll pay you five dollars to stop talking like Gandalf."

"Thank the gods."

The second week of spring break passed in this way. At the end of it, Lewis and Clark College came to town.

Why Can't We Beat You?
Walla Walla, Washington vs The Lewis and Clark College Pioneers

Lewis and Clark was always a team I thought we could beat. It was a delusion that kept me alive. Our schedule was filled with dragons. I knew that Linfield was going to annihilate us. I knew that George Fox was going to annihilate us. I was pretty sure that Pacific Lutheran was going to annihilate us. I needed something to look forward to.

So, I looked forward to Lewis and Clark. My freshman year, they finished last in the conference. We even took two out of three from them. "Well," I concluded. "We will forever be better than Lewis and Clark."

The problem was that Lewis and Clark got better while we got worse. They swept us my sophomore year. They swept us my junior year. Many of the games weren't close, but my belief in our superiority was unshaken. When they came to Walla Walla in late March, I thought that our losing streak was about to end. Then, of course, they swept us again.

The strangest thing is that some part of me is still convinced that we were better than Lewis and Clark, even though our career record against them was 2-11, and they outscored us 60-152.

The Results

Date	Score
3/29/08	Whitman 5 - 12 Lewis and Clark (L)
	Whitman 4 - 12 Lewis and Clark (L)
3/30/08	Whitman 3 - 8 Lewis and Clark (L)
	Whitman 4 - 14 Lewis and Clark (L)

	Record	
W	L	Losing Streak
2	22	21

Bombs Away

Salem, Oregon vs The Willamette University Bearcats

I almost went to Willamette. I visited the campus my senior year of high school. It was nice. There were a lot of trees. The students were friendly. But I didn't love it.

In all honesty, I didn't love Whitman, either. I was too afraid. There were too many people and not enough rules. I ultimately chose Whitman for two reasons: 1) it had a slightly better academic reputation; and 2) my friend went there.

You could say that I rejected Willamette. "It's not you," I told it, "it's me."

"But," I thought to myself, "actually it is you."

So, naturally, I thought we should beat them at baseball. We did. Three times in four years. Of course, that means they beat us ten times in four years, but that's ok.

Senior year they absolutely pounded us. April 5, 2008, marks the single worst day of baseball I have ever been a part of. When in one day you lose two games by a combined total of forty-one runs... well, hopefully you never have a worse day than that.

On the flip side, Willamette catcher Max Stepan had perhaps the best day of his life, going 4-5 in the second game with two homers and nine RBIs. The one thing you could say about us is that we made everyone else better.

The Results

Date	Score
4/05/08	Whitman 1 - 20 Willamette (L)
	Whitman 3 - 25 Willamette (L)
4/06/08	Whitman 6 - 9 Willamette (L)
	Whitman 4 - 8 Willamette (L)

Record

W	L	Losing Streak
2	26	25

REGULAR SEASON—WEEK SIX

Where Is the Bear Mace?

Walla Walla, Washington vs The George Fox University Bruins

George Fox was the other school in the conference with a National Championship. Their baseball homepage lists a string of accomplishments that makes me sick. One NCAA D-III National Championship. Eight National Tournament appearances. Nine Northwest Conference Championships. Nineteen consecutive winning seasons. Twenty-two players signed to pro contracts.

What the hell?

We obviously didn't beat George Fox once in my four years at Whitman. But we did have one thing over them: we could swear.

George Fox is a Christian university, and (the story goes that) swearing is a finable offense there. At Whitman, *not* swearing is a finable offense. When we played George Fox, I think we took a perverse pleasure in striking out because then we could curse under our breath just loudly enough for the catcher to hear.

The best thing about playing at George Fox was the hecklers. I'm not sure why anybody would have heckled us. Heckling us was one step above heckling small children. We were so horrible that the only emotions opposing fans (and probably players) could have felt for us must have been sympathy, embarrassment, and perhaps resentment for wasting their time.

That said, apparently some college-aged males will heckle anything, even if they can't use colorful language.

"You are bad!" They (actually) yelled at us from beyond the outfield fences.

Well, yes, thank you for noticing.

The Results

Date	Score
4/12/08	Whitman 1 – 13 George Fox (L)
	Whitman 2 – 10 George Fox (L)
4/13/08	Whitman 0 – 2 George Fox (L, but, Wow!)
	Whitman 1 – 9 George Fox (L)

Record

W	L	Losing Streak
2	30	29

The Great Schism

Tacoma, Washington vs The Pacific Lutheran University Lutes

At this point, the season had taken a serious psychological toll on me. I remember waking up before the first day of games and feeling seventy-five percent insane. I spent the pregame warm-up in a daze. The air was not quite air. It was more like soup.

It must have been the result of a horrible chemical imbalance in my brain, produced by a prolonged streak of futility combined with the looming uncertainty of graduation. Whatever the cause of my malaise, the last place I wanted to be was on the baseball field.

There came a point where I prayed that I wouldn't be in the lineup. "Please," I thought, "just let me sit on the bench." I almost went up to Casey and told him not to put me in. I thought about telling him that I felt sick. But that would have been a lie. I wasn't sick. I was just on the verge of a mental breakdown. I said nothing.

At one point, he put me in. I walked up to the batter's box, afraid that I would collapse and have a seizure or something. I drew a walk and then stole second base. I was mystified. I told myself that the season was almost over.

The Results

Date	Score
4/19/08	Whitman 3 – 8 Pacific Lutheran (L)
	Whitman 2 – 10 Pacific Lutheran (L)
4/20/08	Whitman 0 – 7 Pacific Lutheran (L)
	Whitman 1 – 13 Pacific Lutheran (L)

Record

W	L	Losing Streak
2	34	33

The End of the Line
Walla Walla, Washington vs The Whitworth University Pirates

Here it was—the last series of the year. I remember sitting in the dugout after warm-ups, looking down at my feet. One of the assistant coaches, a former standout (and future manager) named Kinney, noticed me.

"How are you doing?" he asked.

I try to be a positive person, but I couldn't muster any cheer at that moment. I felt like a cockroach doomed to spend eternity in a crowded kitchen. Inevitably I would be squashed, and inevitably I would be reborn, only to be squashed again.

"I'm sad," I said, without looking up.

I think he knew.

Joe Rodhouse started the first game. Joe was a workhorse, a righty who ate up innings on a team that desperately needed them eaten up. He pitched well, but the game went into the bottom of the seventh with the score Whitworth 4, Whitman 0. It looked like any number of losses we had already suffered that year. Well, actually, it looked a little bit different in that we weren't down by twenty runs yet.

But then something *very* different happened. We started to rally. Dan White led off the 7th with a single. Matt Morris-Rosen ⁃ feld followed with a double. Dan scored, and it was 4-1.

Laz, our catcher from So Cal, followed with a single. Erik Korsmo, freshman dynamo, blasted a double to right. Matt scored, and Laz went to third. It was 4-2. There were no outs, two runs in, and runners on second and third.

It had been such a long time since we'd had any momentum that I almost didn't recognize it. I sat on my bucket near the bench, sucking the flavor off of a mouthful of sunflower seeds. *Are we actually scoring runs?* I spat out a shell and waited for the rally to die.

Then Micah Babbitt singled. Two runners scored, and the game was tied. Austin Shackleford singled. Luke singled. The score was 5-4. We were winning for the first time in months, and we still didn't have any outs. We scored one more run on a single by Nate Rankin.

When the dust of that inning had settled, the score was Whit - man 6, Whitworth 4. And we weren't done. We scored two more in the bottom of the eight on a triple by Shackleford. Joe went back to the mound for the 9th, holding an 8-4 lead.

The inning started off well as Joe got the first guy to ground out, but then the wheels started to wobble. He walked the next batter and gave up back-to-back singles. The bases were loaded with only one out. If they hit a home run, the game would be tied. My knees were knocking, but I was on the bench so my treach - erous thoughts didn't hurt anybody.

Joe got the next guy to fly out. A run scored, making it 8-5. The next batter stepped into the box with two outs and a chance to tie the game.

Joe struck him out. Shockingly, we had won.

I cheered wildly. We all cheered wildly. The fans, all ten of them, cheered wildly. What else were we going to do? We had just broken a thirty-three-game losing streak. I tried to make sense of it. *How should I feel?* I held the futility of the season—of all of the seasons since I had become a Missionary—over my head and then tried to let it go, hoping it would fall off my shoulders and roll down my back.

But it didn't. The thrill of victory lasted for a minute. Then the misery of all the defeats flooded back in. We lost the second game of the doubleheader by a respectable score of 7-5. The next day were the last two games of college baseball I would ever play.

Day One Results

Date	Score
4/26/08	Whitman 8 – 5 Whitworth (W)
	Whitman 5 – 7 Whitworth (L)

Senior Day

Sunday was Senior Day. On Senior Day, it's tradition for the graduating class to go onto the field, line up on one of the base - lines, and have a short piece read about each of them. You could call it their college-baseball obituary. Most are short, sweet, and relatively formulaic: "Billy, a career .290 hitter, will graduate with a major in communications, and aspires to one day work in marketing."

At that point, there were five of us, and we were having none of that. We wanted to break the mold. For one, there would be no mention of statistics (for perhaps obvious reasons). For another, they wouldn't be boring. We were weird and wanted our bios to reflect that. We asked Casey if we could write them. He told us to knock ourselves out. We drew names and then knocked each other out.

Maybe our bios confused the Whitworth players so much that they forgot how to play baseball. We won the first game, this time 3-1. Pete Stadmeyer, a left-handed sophomore and our most consistent pitcher, scattered four hits over seven innings to get his first career win. We shook hands in the infield, and it felt almost normal. A bandage appeared on the gaping wound that was the season. As long as I kept my eye on the final series and didn't peer at the festering sore of failure hiding beneath, I almost felt like a member of a baseball team again.

The second game was more characteristically us. Because it was the last game of the year, all of the seniors started, including me. I put on my helmet and went out to left.

It was a back-and-forth game. Going into the top of the sixth in a seven-inning game, the score was tied 5-5. We went into the field and tried to hold them. The first batter of the inning lined out to Luke in center. Then came back-to-back singles, leaving runners on first and third with one out.

Next up was their number-five hitter. His name was Chad Flett. I don't run into very many Chads, so when I do it's kind of weird. Mike was on the mound. I crept forward. He threw. The other Chad swung, making solid contact. The ball was coming right at me. I was behind it. The runner at third tagged as I reached for the ball, ready to throw home.

And then I didn't catch it. The ball hit my glove and rolled all of the way to the fence. I threw my helmet in disgust as Luke ran to chase the ball. The guy at third scored easily, and then eight other Whitworth players followed. When the inning finally ended, we were down 14-5. We lost 15-7.

The Results

Date	Score
4/27/08	Whitman 3 - 1 Whitworth (W)
	Whitman 7 - 15 Whitworth (L)

Final Record

W	L
4	36

After the game, we had a team barbecue. Two years earlier, one of the parents had made a speech. He stood up as we chewed our hamburgers in silence. "Ten years from now," he said, looking at us with a very real, very proud smile, "No one is going to care what your record was."

I kept chewing. That year our record was 3-35.

"They're going to hear that you played college baseball, and they're going to be impressed."

I appreciated his attempt to make us feel better, but it didn't work, at least not on me.

I don't remember if anybody said anything at our barbecue. I was too lost in my own thoughts to hear.

IV.

———

A WHITMAN BASEBALL PLAYER'S
SEARCH FOR MEANING

Where is the Love?

A FEW WEEKS AFTER THE SEASON ENDED, there was a celebration for senior athletes. We gathered in a big room in Reid Campus Center and sat down for some food and photos. Someone had put together a slideshow, and as the photos cycled through, I found myself smiling. Every time a baseball picture popped up, a memory came with it. We looked at each and laughed.

While the lights were off and the highlight reel played, I found myself steeped in an unfamiliar warmth.

Maybe it was worth it after all?

Then the lights came back on, the athletes scattered, and the warm glow faded. The pain of the futility reasserted itself, collapsing my smile into a scowl.

Thank God it's over, I thought. Baseball faded from my mind, replaced by thoughts of graduation and my impending move to Japan.

Six months later, however, sitting at my desk at a junior high school in Hamamatsu City, baseball was back on my mind. My life was suddenly full of holes, and one of them was shaped like a baseball. I still had no idea what to think of my time on the Whitman team, but one thing was clear: I had to get back my love for the game.

I tried a lot of different things. First, I turned my eyes to the Mariners—who had been almost as bad as we had been while I was at Whitman—and tried to get excited about them again.

But how to do that? I was no longer a ten-year-old looking to his idols. How could I enjoy following the team again? I pondered the question for a while before an idea came to me: Sabermetrics.

I looked up advanced stats, trying to memorize what went into OPS, FIP, and wOBA. I became mildly obsessed with WAR tables and read message boards where people bashed the establish - ment for relying on something as antiquated as their eyes and ears.

That was interesting, but it wasn't what I was looking for. I appreciate math but looking at numbers I didn't understand wasn't like unwrapping a black and white TPX bat on Christmas morning.

The Other End of the Dugout

I was finished as a player, and I hadn't found a hard-core fan in myself, either. But maybe there was a coach? The school where I worked had a very serious baseball team. I wondered if being with the players might rekindle my flame.

I asked the baseball coach if I could come to practice. He was very welcoming, so one day I brought my glove to school and after class walked ten minutes to the patch of dirt they called home.

The way the kids approached baseball was awe-inspiring. Even though the oldest were only fifteen, they went to the field and warmed up on their own. They stretched. They played catch. They bowed and apologized to the rest of the team every time they made an error. I had never seen anything like it.

Sadly, I was still too shell-shocked to really enjoy it. When I watched them yell and hustle around their diamond, I couldn't help thinking, "This will all end badly." I didn't see *them*. I saw my younger self. I knew what awaited him: Loggers, Lutes, Wildcats, and Bruins, ready to chew him up and spit him out.

After a few trips to the field, I thanked the coach and stopped going.

When I got back to Seattle five years later, I thought I would try again. I emailed the varsity coach at Shorecrest and asked if the JV team could use an assistant. Maybe putting on the green and gold would help me recover what I had lost?

When I showed up, I saw that the field was different. The dirt cutouts and lumpy green grass were gone, replaced by soothingly regular field turf. Medalia and Woodward were also gone, along with all of my other coaches.

A lot of things were the same, however. The woods still swallowed foul balls. The batting cages were still slabs of concrete carpeted with old turf. I recognized the stack of tires we had used to keep the tarps in place, and they still used the long, green shipping containers to house the rakes and the Diamond Dry. Ten years had passed, but the sight of the field brought back a lot of memories.

One in particular stood out. It was senior year, and Medalia had gathered us into a circle. "One day," he said, attempting to break through our teenaged barriers with a fierce stare, "You're going to be old."

Here we go again, I remember thinking.

"When you look back on your high school days," he continued, "you're not going to miss most of it. Hell," he said, a gleam coming into his eye, "you're not even going to remember most of it."

Medalia's gaze bore into one player after another as he paused to let the message sink in. "But you are going to remember the time you spent on this field."

Breathing in the wet spring air a decade later, I realized that he had been right about that last part.

The JV team was great. The head coach was full of energy, the players were fun, and I enjoyed my time with them. The baseball itself, however, was blah. It wasn't because of the way they played it, of course. It was just that my love of the game had been mostly ground away.

Finally, after all of the effort, I was forced to admit something that I'd known for a long time. It wasn't just that I didn't love baseball anymore; I hated it.

There is the Love

I HATE BASEBALL.

It felt right. Even the part of me that had—for years—been holding onto its identity as a baseball player agreed.

How could I love baseball when I took a beating every time I played?

I couldn't. It was a relief to finally stop trying.

When I did, clarity followed.

Why had I loved baseball as a kid? On the one hand, it had given me a place to meet and hang out with friends. On the other hand, it had also given me a place to be of value to those friends. Until Whitman, I could hit, field, run and throw well enough to help my teams win.

Baseball, however, is a competitive sport, which means nobody is guaranteed victory. In my neck of the woods, most boys played when they were in Little League. You could say that the competition wasn't terribly fierce. As we got older, those who weren't great at the game dropped out. With time, only the best and most dedicated played on. By the time I was in college, selection pressures had weeded out almost everyone I had ever played with.

My position at Whitman was unique. At almost any other college, I wouldn't have been good enough to sneak onto the team. At Whitman, however, I made the cut because there wasn't one. Our opponents were in a different situation. They were real college baseball players, so I couldn't compete with them.

From the outside, this probably sounds very obvious. From the inside, however, it was hard to accept.

What do you mean I'm not good enough?

Don't you know who I am?

When I was twelve, I had been David taking down Goliath. Some part of me had wanted to play that role forever. By the end of my time at Whitman, however, a parade of Goliaths had pounded that part of me into dust.

Ten years have passed since then, and when I look at the empty pedestal where my heroic baseball self once stood, I see something surprising: I am OK without him. I don't have to be a giant-killer to be happy in the world—which is a relief, because I'm not really qualified for that role anyway.

I also realize that I was OK at Whitman, too. I was a bad player and we were the complete doormat of the league, and yet when I look away from the stats, I notice that I loved my time on the team. The games themselves weren't very much fun, but the time in between them usually was.

I loved doing infield drills with Adam, tossing our gloves aside and trying to pick the ball out of the dirt with our bare hands. I loved going to the gym after class and pretending that I knew how to lift weights. I loved going to Reid Campus Center after practice and eating bacon-cheeseburgers (I didn't need to pretend I knew how to do that).

The best thing about the team was all of the characters. You've read a fair amount about some of them, but there were many more, and each contributed his own unique something. Mo-Ro contributed his enthusiasm and *Wedding Crashers* DVD. Pearsall brought the wisdom of old age and a set of ridiculous red contact lenses, Spence-Mo brought a healthy supply of peanut butter and jelly sandwiches, and JD graced us with doubles to the gap and belly flops at first base.

I spent years looking for my love of the game, but in writing this book I eventually found it right where it had always been: in the dugout, on the bus, and between the lines with my friends.

So, what did baseball teach me about life? There were the early lessons, of course. Few people appreciate excuses. Attitude and hustle are important. Some of the limitations we place on ourselves—based on body size, for example—are imaginary.

The later lessons were more painful but also deeper. Ultimately, baseball taught me that some of our limitations are very real. At the same time, it also taught me that I could survive even the most brutal dismantling of my own self-image, and that close friendships can redeem utter futility.

Those are lessons very much worth having learned. The speech at the year-end BBQ rings differently with them in my ear.

"Ten years from now," that father said, "nobody will care about your record. They'll hear that you played college baseball and they will be impressed."

He was partially right. If I were to rewrite his speech, it would go a little differently.

*Ten years from now, **you** won't care about your record. You'll remember the times you spent with each other, and you will be happy to have been on the team.*

That's a peg I can hang my spikes on.

Epilogue

The Rise of the Missionaries—I Mean the Blues

I graduated from Whitman in 2008. As you now know, we were not good.

But where is the team in 2019?

I'm happy and a little bit shocked to report that they are well on their way to respectability. This is in large part thanks to two of my former teammates: Sean Kinney and Brian Kitamura.

Kinney was one of the best players I'd ever played with. He became the interim head coach in 2013. That year the team went 16-22. In the 2014 season, they actually had a winning record: 20-18-1. I can't quite believe that that is possible.

Brian—we knew him as BK—took over for Kinney in 2015. He holds the distinction of being one of the kindest people ever to put on a Whitman uniform. Since he took over, the Whitman mascot has changed to the Blues, after a nearby mountain range. Their record through the 2018 season was 54-93, very solid for a Whitman team. Shockingly, they seem to have swept George Fox in three games in 2018, but I don't believe that that is possible either. In fact, it gets even better. The day before I wrote this in the spring of 2019, the Blues punched their ticket to the North - west Conference tournament for the first time in school history, with two wins against Lewis and Clark (I knew we were better than them). The Blues finished the season 20-16, which earned them an astounding second place in the conference. It turns out that sometimes miracles do happen.

In the fall of 2018, I got to experience their transformation first-hand. I was in Walla Walla for my ten-year reunion, but the alumni baseball game happened to be on the same weekend.

The alumni baseball game is held every fall. Former Whitman baseballers from across the decades come back to Walla Walla to play a game or two against the current squad. I had never played in one as an alum. I had been in Japan for a number of my years post-graduation, yes, but for four years I had been in Seattle. For reasons you might now appreciate, I'd never felt motivated to make the drive east.

This year, however, it was time.

Luke and I walked from our rental house to DeSales. The field was packed with ballplayers from age eighteen to fifty-five, most of whom I did not know. Dan White was there, along with Andrew Shultz, the man who once caught a ball at the wall for another team's home run. It was a pleasant surprise to see them both.

A pair of large Tupperware containers sat on the bench in the first-base dugout. One was filled with old blue jerseys, the other with old gray pants. I fished out a jersey and a pair of pants and put them on without a belt. I didn't have cleats, so I stepped onto the field in bright blue running shoes.

Luke and I went down the right field line to warm up, and I was happy to find that I could still catch. I was happier to find that my shoulder didn't hurt very much when I threw. When it was time to take warm-ups, I went out to second base. I didn't have a helmet, but I did have a smile my face.

The game began after warm-ups. There were around thirty-five alumni, and I was roughly thirtieth in the batting order. With twenty-seven outs in a nine-inning game, there was no guarantee I would get to hit. Luckily a few old-timers got on base, so in the late innings I stepped into the box for my first at-bat in ten years.

I decided to swing as hard as I could at the first pitch. The pitcher wound up and threw. I let it rip. Halfway through the swing my left shoulder popped part-way out of its socket. I missed by a mile and stumbled into the left-hand batter's box, cradling my arm.

"I dislocated my shoulder on that one," I chuckled as I sheep - ishly returned to the right-hand batter's box. The catcher either didn't hear me or ignored me.

My shoulder had immediately re-located itself, but my arm was numb, so I couldn't have swung at the next pitch if I had wanted to. It went by for strike two. I was determined to swing at the next one, no matter what the effect on my ligaments.

The pitcher threw another fastball and I swung—and made contact! Barely. The ball dribbled towards the pitcher and I took off for first base.

"Hard ninety!"

I heard Van Dyke's voice in my head as I sprinted down the line. I was out by thirty feet, but managed not to collapse in a heap as I went by the base.

The current squad beat us handily, which is as it should have been. There was a second game, but Luke and I decided we had played enough double-headers wearing Whitman jerseys. We walked back to the rental house for cold beer and a hot shower.

Words from Whitties

I asked some of my teammates and coaches for their own thoughts on Whitman baseball. Here is what they had to say.

Adam Knappe
Heartbreak, Humility, and Humor

I played college baseball for four seasons at Whitman. I underwent psychotherapy for two of those seasons.

Let me put it frankly—these were troubling times. I, like Chad, had spent my childhood worshipping at the church of baseball. And most importantly, I was the devout parishioner-practitioner. I played every chance I got—on city teams, traveling teams, off-season tournaments, backyard Wiffle ball, and on and on. If there were objects that could be used as ball and bat, and a few other kids to play with, I was there. I loved the game, and, for the most part, was successful at it. And I loved being successful at it.

Whitman baseball changed this narrative. We were almost never successful. In fact, we were consistently unsuccessful. We were so unsuccessful that I would often arrive to a visiting ball - park for the first of our weekend's games and feel like we'd already lost by the time we took the field for batting practice. (It didn't help things that Central Washington University once infa -

mously played the Aqua song "Barbie Girl" when it was our turn to hit.)

It still feels like something of an accident that I got to play college baseball—after all, I wasn't a particularly noticeable talent nor was I healthy for most of my high school senior season. But I *did* play college baseball.

That said, as we continued to lose, many of my expectations of myself—and in particular, my belief in my capabilities on and off the field—withered. I struggled with confidence, self-esteem, and self-doubt. My dating life was an "0-fer," and it sometimes felt worse than our team's losing streaks. But I kept playing ball.

And now that I look back, I have zero regrets. I made incredible friends. And after all, I can say that I was a college baseball player! (One of my colleague's favorite jokes is that I played D5 baseball...) I look back on my years of Whitman baseball fondly.

I'll be honest—in my childhood, baseball taught me that I was an unrequited "winner." Whitman baseball taught me something much more useful. It taught me the humility to realize that I'm a loser, a winner, and everything in-between.

Luke Marshall
Keeping it Between the Lines

Rather than write a single all-encompassing something, I'm going to recount two stories. Each anecdote, in its own way, perfectly encapsulates my Whitman Baseball experience.

First, a memory from the field (recounted by Chad earlier)—although calling what I'm about to recount a "memory," might be a little shaky medically speaking, considering the result was my first (mild) concussion.

I have, and will always, maintain two fundamental truths about "The Wall" incident: (1) I got a fantastic jump on the ball and, given its hang time, had a legitimate shot at catching it; and (2) Dan White, our freshman centerfielder, failed to warn me that I was bearing down on the outfield wall a lot faster than on the ball.

For what it's worth, Dan has always counter-claimed that (1) not even Griffey in his prime could have caught that ball, it was hit so deep, and (2) ... yeah, he doesn't really have a response other than to refer me back to his first point.

Because I had no vocal warning from my centerfielder, and the literal warning track (that gravel section leading up to the wall on any decent baseball field) was so short, I was running at a full sprint.

Luckily, (as Chad alluded to earlier) my full sprint was, well, less than sprinty.

Unluckily, I still had a lot of momentum.

Luckily, it was a chain-link fence, not brick.

Unluckily, I hit a post instead of the chain-link.

This cadence sums up Whitman baseball pretty well: "not-bad" was about as lucky as we got; our bad luck was down-right shitty.

But then why did we play? Or at the very least, why did I play?

The best articulation I ever gave of this was probably in response to a friend of mine—Matt Aliabadi—who asked: "Why are you doing this to yourself?" after yet another loss, probably during our junior year.

My explanation at the time, which I still I believe, was something close to the following:

For me, playing baseball was an escape—even if while playing for Whitman it was an escape to a shitty place. Regardless of the outcome, every time you lace up and step between the lines, the only way you can possibly have a good outcome is if everything else stays outside of those lines. Bullshit with school, bullshit with your girlfriend, and even legitimate things that *should* be getting you down as a normal sane person—if you bring it on the field, you will definitely fail.

So, baseball becomes its own world, with well-understood rules. It's always easy to see who won and lost the pitch, the at-bat, the inning, and the game. It is a self-contained creation of meaning and purpose.

That meaning and purpose is unintelligible from the outside. The outcome of a baseball game objectively does not matter in the real world. But getting on the field is no longer the real world. That's the point.

So, no matter what was going on in my life, I had three hours (or six on our double-header days) in which I was *required* to not think about anything outside of this fantasy land. Literally the only thing in the world that matters there is winning the pitch, the at-bat, the inning and the game.

In our case, we just sucked at doing that thing. But in the striving and failing there was still an escape from everyday life, where it can be harder to find concrete purpose and meaning. Plus, there was also a little bit of pathetic beauty in sucking at it together.

My friend's response to that was basically: "Actually, I totally understand that. What I do as a hobby (improv) requires you to bring all your baggage and bullshit with you. Stepping outside it for a while sounds nice."

So... we got to step outside of our normal life bullshit for a while. The fact that the alternate universe we participated in also had a pasture-like aroma wasn't really the point.

On a sappier note, this group of guys was the best. Some unsolicited advice: if you're opting to pursue a shitty and point - less undertaking, at least do it with funny people. That way you'll still be cracking each other up about it ten years later.

Sam Thompson
Calm, Collected, and Psychologically Healthy

For me, Whitman baseball was a great experience. The friendships and memories I made while living, practicing, traveling, and playing with my teammates will likely stay with me the rest of my life. What a unique, wacky, and intelligent group of guys—there was never a dull moment!

But what about all the losing, you ask? Didn't I feel a deep sense of despair that we could hardly win any games all four years? Yes, losing sucks and I definitely felt a certain level of frustration with that. But I really didn't feel a deep despair like I think a lot of my teammates did. I think I handled it better for two main reasons.

First, losing was nothing new to me. I can only remember a couple of times in all my years playing baseball when I played on a winning team (Was it me?). My high school team reliably won only a few games each season and lost big-time in the rest of them. So, I was used to losing more than winning. Plus, I knew Whitman was not an athletic powerhouse going in—most of us were there because of its academic reputation, not its prowess in sports—so I really had no big expectations to win.

Second, I arrived at Whitman with an easygoing personality and an upbringing that did not put much emphasis (if any) on winning. My parents were always very supportive of my baseball endeavors—I don't think my mom ever missed a game—but I never got the sense that they cared <u>at all</u> whether my team won or lost. They were happy I was playing and proud of me no matter what, so I felt the same way. I learned from them not to tie my self-worth to winning or losing, so it was just never that important to me in the long run to win.

Don't get me wrong—it's not that I am not competitive. In the heat of the moment, when I'm on the field, I want to win that game. I can even be extremely frustrated right after a loss, espe - cially when it's a game we should have won. But at the end of the day, I have never dwelled on that result for long. I let things go. That trait, combined with the perspective that winning was not a reflection of my self-worth, allowed me to weather the storms of Whitman baseball, perhaps better than most of my teammates.

So, what did I take from my Whitman baseball experience? First, foremost, and most valuable are those bonds I developed and the memories. If you asked me to trade all of that to play on a different, winning team, I would say, No Deal! I treasure the experiences I had much more than I would a collection of winning seasons absent the camaraderie and friendships.

Kramer Phillips
Knowing When to Move on

Chad asked me about the despair I felt playing at Whitman, but it is difficult to define it as despair—in retrospect, at the end of the day it was just baseball. I would say it was more of a persis - tent feeling of failure, which seemed to heavily weigh on me as the months wore on. I always enjoyed the early days of the season. (Unlike others, I never had hope we would win; instead, I simply love that time of the year and getting back on the field.) However, by the time the first few weeks were under our belt, and we had inevitably lost a lot of games, I was pretty much over it. For people who enjoy competing, losing as often as we did was especially disheartening. I don't think I ever found the time spent with the team unenjoyable, but I am not someone who enjoys losing (even a tiny bit), so Whitman baseball, as time passed, was less and less of a priority.

At the end of the day, I am not sure what could have or should have changed to make the entire experience all that much better. By the time I hit college, I was already in post-baseball mode and interested in spending my time on pursuits other than those on the field. I think if I had seen more reasons to invest time (summer baseball leagues, for example), I might have continued playing, but I can't be sure.

Chad also asked me what I learned from playing at Whitman. The main thing was that I do not enjoy losing. By the time I hit Whitman, I had learned quite a bit through baseball, so I view the time at Whitman as more of a "setting sun" phase. As those who have played baseball know, the game is as much about failure as it is about success. I think that was especially (sometimes brutally) true with Whitman. That said, all sports have their big losers (see: Cleveland Browns), so I don't think that was particu - larly unique to Whitman baseball.

Overall, I learned a great deal more from my time playing before Whitman. Above all, I would say the ability to effectively absorb failures and move on is the most important lesson I took from playing. Early on, I would also say it showed the value of hard work and how practicing something can actually result in change.

Casey Powell
Working the Phones, Raking the Ruts

Chad asked me about the challenges of coaching at Whitman. The challenges there were normal challenges of other small-college coaches, but sometimes we had some circumstances that made it more difficult.

Budget was a big factor; our budget was smaller than what it cost to attend Whitman in a calendar year. With a budget that small, there was fundraising that had to be done but a lot of the hang-ups that came with fundraising were players wanting to know why they needed to do fundraising when the school tuition cost so much.

Recruiting was always difficult; it wasn't typically the admission piece that most people would think. I felt like I did a good job of identifying athletes who academically could meet the challenges of a Whitman education, and then encouraged them to apply. The most difficult part was the financial aid—making it affordable for their parents to send them to Whitman. It was frustrating working so hard to get kids to apply and want to come to the college but not being able to because of the lack of aid.

The facilities were never great when I was there, either; the indoor facility was small and limited what we could do, and the field was never great. Despite how hard I worked with the head groundskeeper at the field, it was never where I wanted it to be.

Chad also asked me about the positives of coaching at Whitman. I have always enjoyed working with student-athletes, and I have been fortunate to work at some institutions where the athletes did honestly care about their education. This was something I always respected about the Whitman students; most were able to see the bigger picture and had a focus of where their future was and what they wanted to do.

I always appreciated that the student-athletes I worked with would be coming from lab or a class and immediately be ready to practice and work. I believe that some of the players understood that this was a place to get away from the books and studies for a brief time and enjoy it with some friends.

I have enjoyed hearing from former players and how they are doing; it is usually a positive conversation.

Coach Van Dyke

The Man Himself

I spent four seasons working with young men who weren't much younger than I was. These men taught me more than I probably taught them on and off the field. I look back now after eleven more seasons of coaching baseball and wish I could have done more for them as players. I stay in contact with some that are still in the area and they have turned out to be great men. I am happy to see the program heading in the right direction; Coach K is a great guy and is doing great things at Whitman.

Also, I just want to say I am a lot better at throwing BP now!

Stats

Outstanding Outcomes

Date	Score
4/03/05	Whitman 5 – 20 Whitworth
3/22/05	Whitman 2 – 27 George Fox
4/06/05	Whitman 1 – 24 Central Washington
3/26/06	Whitman 4 – 29 Linfield
4/14/06	Whitman 2 – 22 Willamette
3/19/06	Whitman 6 – 25 George Fox
2/18/06	Whitman 6 – 25 Cal State Eastbay
3/11/07	Whitman 0 – 20 George Fox
3/21/08	Whitman 0 – 23 Pacific
4/05/08	Whitman 1 – 20 Willamette
4/05/08	Whitman 3 – 25 Willamette

My 2008 stat line

Batting Average	.146
Strike-Out Percentage	31%
RBIs	4

My Career Whitman Stat Line

Batting Average	.176
On Base Percentage	.288
Plate Appearances	153
Hits	27
Strike Outs	41
Walks	17
Hit by Pitch	7

Endnotes

1. I wore a helmet in the field that year. I'll tell you why in chapter eight.
2. With the notable exception of the 2001 season, when they won the most regular season games in major league history (and then lost in the second round of the playoffs).
3. Legendary Mariners' announcer.
4. He was coaching my younger brother.
5. His groovy mane of dark, curly hair probably didn't hurt the association.
6. My kart was the much more sophisticated "Godforce."
7. In this book I will refer to him only as Woodward. This, while disrespectful, most faithfully represents our eighteen-year-old attitudes.
8. In Washington these labels are based on the size of the student population. 4A was the largest category at the time.
9. Clete had an unbelievable senior season—halfway through, his batting average was over .600. He finished near .440.
10. Sort of.
11. George Fox won the D-III national championship in 2004, the year before I went to Whitman.
12. Reflections from Casey and a number of the Whitman players from my class are collected at the end of the book. I really enjoyed reading them and hope you will, too.
13. So, I suppose it was almost as if they had gone to a strip club.
14. At that point it was too late for me to learn anything about baseball anyway.
15. Sam confirms that his batting average was .487 and that his no-hitter was thrown against fully sighted players.

16. .316 his junior year, with 24 RBIs.
17. I'm happy to report that Whitman baseball did not actually render him impotent. His wife gave birth to a boy in 2016.

Colophon

This book was designed and developed by Dana Johnson in Markdown and CSS using a modified version of Chris Ferdinandi's EBook Boilerplate and the open source document converters Pandoc and WeasyPrint. The text is set in the open source typeface family IBM Plex.

CHAD FRISK was a serious baseball player from the age of five to twenty-two. His career batting average would be much higher if you removed his last four seasons. He currently lives in Seattle, WA and occasionally plays beer league softball.

Made in the USA
Lexington, KY
26 April 2019